How *Sovereign* is Your God?

How sovereign is Your God? Was a great reminder for me of how God moves in our lives. Just as He moved in the lives of some of the great heroes of the Bible – very thought provoking! I enjoyed doing the lessons by myself, but I am looking forward to studying it together with other believers. I'm sure we can help each other grow in our spiritual walk through the discussion questions and by looking up the various scriptures. I love a Bible study that has you looking up scripture after scripture. What a way to grow!

~ *Patty Shaffer*

How Sovereign is Your God?

A Bible Study
Exploring the Sovereignty
of God by Looking at
the Heroes of the Faith

For Personal or Small Group Study

Debbie Blough

Debbie Blough

TATE PUBLISHING & Enterprises

IS 44:6-8

Published by Tate Publishing & Enterprises, LLC
127 E. Trade Center Terrace | Mustang, Oklahoma 73064 USA
1.888.361.9473 | www.tatepublishing.com

Tate Publishing is committed to excellence in the publishing industry. The company reflects the philosophy established by the founders, based on Psalm 68:11,
"The Lord gave the word and great was the company of those who published it."

Book design copyright © 2009 by Tate Publishing, LLC. All rights reserved.
Cover design by Kristen Polson
Interior design by Janae J. Glass

Published in the United States of America

ISBN: 978-1-60696-383-8
1. Religion/Biblical Reference
2. General
09.02.12

Many times during the writing of this book I received, what I believed to be, confirmations from God. Many times I would be working on a chapter and would hear a sermon about that same topic. One day as I was talking with a group of ladies from my church one of the women said word for word a sentence that I had just written hours before.

The final confirmation I received came through my daughter. The book was nearing completion and Cindy came home from high school with this painting, which she had completed in art class. Unbeknownst to Cindy at the time I was contemplating a cover for the book. I knew at once that God had given me the concept for the cover.

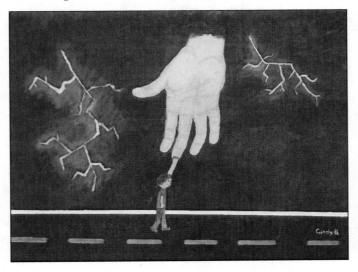

Psalm 139:10 Even there Your hand will lead me, And Your right hand will lay hold of me.

Acknowledgments

I am grateful to the triune God for revealing Himself to me and for the salvation of my soul. I thank-you Lord for showing me Your sovereignty, growing my faith, and helping me to live a victorious life. All praise, honor, and glory go to Him for anything that is valuable in this book.

To my wonderful husband who supports me in all of my endeavors, thanks for sharing your life with me these past twenty-six years!

To my children, thanks for encouraging me and having faith in what God is doing in my life. You guys are truly a wonderful blessing from God above and I am so thankful to Him that you share my faith.

My gratitude to Jan Priddy of Precept Ministries for reviewing the theological content of this book. Also, a debt of gratitude goes to Susan Lakin for her editing services.

To Patty Fink, thanks so much for your friendship and your excitement about this project. Thanks for listening to my ideas, reading each chapter, and for your suggestions for improvement.

Thanks to Susie Harshbarger, Patty Shaffer, Sharon Klein, and Kathy Will for taking time to actually complete this Bible study. All of your feedback and encouragement was very valuable to me.

Lastly, thanks to Tate Publishing for everything you have done to bring this book to completion.

How sovereign is your God ...
Table of Contents

Foreword

One of the most central themes to the Christian faith is the sovereignty of God. The biblical teaching that God is king and supreme ruler over all is essential to the Christian faith.

The understanding of God's sovereignty is the foundation for Christians to stand firm in the midst of turmoil, anxiety, and fear. It is the unmovable belief that God is in control. That God still sits on the throne today. That God still desires that intimate relationship with his created people.

For centuries theologians have debated between divine sovereignty and human responsibility. These concepts seem almost paradoxical. They are difficult for the human mind to grasp let alone comprehend.

Debbie conquers this challenge in this book. She brings this vague Biblical doctrine to easy understanding through biblical examples, personal stories, and a diligent search through God's Word.

Understanding this concept enables one to enjoy life and the blessings God gives even in the midst of strife and heartache. A practice of this doctrine in one's life provides an unshakable faith in the uncertainty of today's ever-changing culture.

Debbie is a living example of this unshakable faith. Debbie, her husband (Roger), and children (Billy and Cindy) live that kind of faith - steadfast, hope filled, uncontrollably devoted, persistent and dedicated. And you can too!

Scott T. Ream
Senior Pastor, Somerset Alliance Church

Preface

Who is your God? Is He the triune God of the Bible? What role does He play in your life? Is He sovereign enough to handle all problems at all times? Is He just a little God to you who is somewhat impotent and may or may not be able to handle your concerns, or is He such a big God that there is nothing He cannot do? Is He responsible for the good in your life, or is He just a God whom you turn to in times of crises?

Several years ago a desire to study God's word and to understand it manifested itself in my life. Shortly thereafter God introduced me to a way of studying scripture known as the inductive method. In this method of study you ask who, what, when, where, why, and how questions of the text. You also mark key words and slow down as you interact with the passages you are studying. As I implemented this method of study, the words of scripture began to take on clarity. This has led not only to an increase of knowledge about God and His Word, but also to an explosion in my faith. My God went from being a sometimes-impotent being, to the all-sufficient, all-knowing, trustworthy God who deserves my complete confidence. He went from a God of chance, to a God who directs all that happens around me.

I believe there are many Christians trying to handle the pressures of daily life in their own strength, failing to understand that the God of the Bible stands ready to take the pressures onto Himself, thereby freeing them to enjoy all He has for them. They are like I was before I came to realize just how sovereign God is.

In this book the reader will take a trip through the pages of God's word. The importance of looking up scriptures is emphasized. This book is not meant to merely give you my view of God's sovereignty. This book should be used in conjunction with your Bible so you may thereby discover what God Himself reveals about His sovereignty through the pages of His holy book. All the scriptures that you are asked to look up are printed in the appendix for your convenience. It is my prayer that as you take this journey you will discover just how sovereign God is and that this discovery will change your life as it has mine.

According to *Webster's Dictionary*, the word sovereign means "above or superior to all others," or "supreme in power, rank, or authority." If God is sovereign, we need to ask the questions: "what is He sovereign over?" and "how does His sovereignty affect my life?" You will notice the word sovereign contains the little word "reign." Over what does God reign? Many Christians would say God is sovereign, that He is supreme in power over everything, but when disaster strikes in their life they question whether or not God is in control. Or when God asks them to do a difficult thing they many times say "no" to God because they fail to see how He can help them to accomplish the seemingly impossible. So, let us take a journey together through God's word, looking at the lives of many of the heroes of faith and see if we can determine if your God is as sovereign as He says He is.

May God richly bless your life as you open His Word!

1

How sovereign is your God ...
On the road map of life?

Where am I? Should I turn around? Maybe at this next intersection I will find the correct road. Could it be I have gone too far? Maybe I have not gone far enough. Possibly I took a wrong turn. There is a good chance I am hopelessly lost. Perhaps I should turn on the GPS system.

There are many navigational tools available today, from the old standard paper road map to a high tech GPS device. These tools are designed to help you get from where you are to where you want to be. These tools are unable to assist you, however, if you do not utilize them.

The GPS system on your dash has no value if it is turned off while you drive aimlessly through a maze of unknown roads. It is not until you turn the unit on and follow its directions that it becomes useful.

There is a journey we are all taking. It is the journey called life. You may know it as the daily grind, the vicious cycle, or the treadmill. You may just be on the first leg of your journey, or you may be nearing the finish line. No matter where you are on your journey or by what name you call it, there is a navigational tool that can help you reach the proper destination successfully. This navigational tool is the Bible and just like the GPS system in your car, the more you use your Bible, the more it will be able to assist you through life.

In this first chapter we are going to look at the overview of life. We will try to answer the question: what is involved in living life well and making wise choices? Then, throughout the rest of the book, we will explore specific situations where you may find yourself and how a sovereign God affects each one.

You may have heard life referred to as a rat race. Just as we sometimes refer to life as a race, the writer of the letter of Hebrews also uses the metaphor of a race to describe the Christian life.

READ HEBREWS 12:1- 2.

What are the two things we must lay aside in order to run the race well?

_____

_____

_____

_____

The first thing mentioned is our encumbrances. An encumbrance is anything that hinders us. It is anything that makes us take our eyes off of the goal we are racing toward. The passage above tells us the goal in this race of the Christian life is Jesus Christ. We are to fix our eyes on Him. We have so many things vying for our time and attention in this fast paced world we live in. What do you fix your attention on during a normal week of your life? Is your attention fixed on Jesus or does He just get whatever time and energy exists at the end of a stressful day? Take a few moments and list some things you feel are encumbrances which hinder you in this race of the Christian life.

_____

_____

_____

_____

_____

_____

_____

_____

_____

The Hebrews passage also tells us we must lay aside the sin that so easily entangles us. Throughout the book of Hebrews the author talks about a specific sin that has devastating results. This sin has the ability to get you thrown into hell for all eternity. If you commit this sin there is no hope. A sin with such dire consequences demands our attention. What is the unpardonable sin? It is the sin of unbelief in Jesus Christ. Jesus says, "I am the way, and the truth, and the life; no one comes to the Father, but through me" (John 14:6). The Bible makes it very clear that Jesus is the only way to heaven. To reject Jesus is to reject heaven. Fortunately, everyone reading this book still has time to accept Him. As long as you have breath in your body it is not too late. If you have never accepted Christ as your savior do so today for none of us knows the length of our days or what tomorrow may bring.

Maybe you are reading this book and you are already a Christian bound for glory. Praise the Lord! What does the sin of unbelief have to do with you? Can a Christian commit a sin of unbelief? The answer may surprise you. Yes, a Christian can commit a sin of unbelief. Notice I said, "a sin" of unbelief not "the sin" of unbelief. There is a difference. While a Christian cannot commit "the sin" of unbelief because the Holy Spirit dwells inside, he can commit "a sin" of unbelief. When we fail to trust God, when we fail to take God at His word then we are committing "a sin" of unbelief. God says, "I will never desert you, nor will I ever forsake you" (Hebrews 13:5). If God is sovereign over all and promises to always be with us then why do we fear? Why do we fret? Why do we fail to run with our eyes fixed on Him? We fail because we have unbelief. I am hoping as you step through the pages in this book you will come to see just how trustworthy and in control God is. Then you will be able to lay aside the sin of unbelief and run the race in a way that is pleasing to Him.

We are on the journey of life. Just as a road map shows many routes to complete your trip, life also presents different roads to travel. There are bends in the road, which are hard to see around. There are dangers lurking everywhere. There are smooth as glass super highways and dirt roads filled with potholes and ruts. How do we choose? We all make choices. We all have plans. We all have dreams we would like to see fulfilled. How do we make choices, devise plans and dream dreams which are pleasing in God's sight?

READ JAMES 4:13–17.
If you read these verses carefully, you will discover the making of plans is not the problem in and of itself. Rather, making plans with the presumption that we are in control of how long we are going to live is the issue. We need to make our

plans, but in humility, knowing God may need to redirect them to accomplish His purposes. Our plans should also be in harmony with God's will. Romans 8:29 tells us that God's will is for us to be conformed to the image of His Son.

READ 1 PETER 4:11

According to this verse what is to be the aim of everything we do?

_____

_____

_____

_____

_____

When you are making plans it is vitally important to make sure everything you plan to do will bring glory to God. Is God glorified when we make plans purely from a selfish motive? Is He glorified when we spend money we do not have to buy things we do not need? Is He glorified when we waste exorbitant amounts of time doing things that have no eternal significance? Does He receive any glory when we go to great lengths to make sure we live in comfort and ease while all around us there are people living in despair and hopelessness? How does God view the person who does not glorify Him with their life?

READ LUKE 12:16–21.

Why does God call this man a fool? Verse twenty-one says it is because he is not rich toward God. He is not running the race with his eyes fixed on Jesus. Instead his eyes are fixed on his wealth and his happiness in the moment. He is concentrating on being merry. He is focused on his flesh. I believe we see this all around us. The endless pursuit for the bigger house, the better job, the faster car, etc. I like how James MacDonald describes a fool. He says:

Do you know what a fool is? A fool is a person who walks through life inattentively. Such a person doesn't weigh their choices but decides on a whim. They wander through life saying, "Well, I think I'll go over here. No, now this other thing is interesting to me; but that third thing is what I want to do with my life!" That's a fool—no discernment or discernible course to life. A fool is almost completely controlled by momentary feelings. A fool fails to realize that some decisions lead to happiness and joy and peace while other decisions lead to heartbreak and misery and devastation.

A foolish person is a person who habitually and sometimes deliberately is oblivious to the rules of life. Such a person drives over a cliff and is surprised and even resentful about the results.[1]

I don't know about you, but I definitely prefer *not* to be called a fool by the all-knowing, all-seeing, sovereign God of the universe. The opposite of a fool is a wise person. The book of Proverbs is known as the book of wisdom. Fifty-eight times the word "wise" appears, and forty-nine times you will see the word "wisdom." If you want to learn what it means to be wise just read through the book of Proverbs and make a list of all the things it says about being wise or having wisdom. Let's take some time and look at a few right now. Read the following passages and then write out the characteristic of a wise person as mentioned in the passage.

PROVERBS 1:5

_____

_____

_____

_____

_____

PROVERBS 9:10

_____

_____

_____

_____

_____

PROVERBS 10:19

_____

_____

_____

_____

_____

PROVERBS 11:2

_____

_____

_____

_____

_____

PROVERBS 12:15

_____

_____

_____

_____

_____

PROVERBS 18:15

_____

_____

_____

_____

PROVERBS 19:20

_____

_____

_____

_____

PROVERBS 29:8

_____

_____

_____

_____

There are many other passages in scripture that talk about wisdom besides those in the book of Proverbs. One such passage is Ephesians 5:15–17. In this passage Paul says, "Therefore, be careful how you walk, not as unwise men, but as wise, making the most of your time, because the days are evil. So then do not be foolish, but understand what the will of the Lord is." Are you being careful how you walk through life? Or are you stumbling along, missing the correct road, and ending up on a detour or dead end? God wants us to be wise and understand His will for our lives. As we obey His will, we "buy up the opportunities" (redeem the time, verse sixteen) and do not waste time, energy, money, and talent in that which is apart from His will. Lost opportunities may never be regained; they are gone forever.[2]

As a parent I wanted my children to possess wisdom as they grew up. In Sept. of 2002 I was listening to a sermon by Charles Stanley. He was preaching about the prayer found in Colossians 1:9–14. He urged every parent to pray that prayer daily for his or her children. So on that September day in 2002, I started praying that prayer for my children and I have continued to this day. I do not pray the prayer word for word but I paraphrase it and ask God for the following things for my kids:

- that they would grow in their knowledge of Him
- that they would be filled with spiritual wisdom
- that they would discover God's will for their lives
- that they would walk in a way that is pleasing to God

At the writing of this book my children are eighteen and twenty-years old. I have witnessed God answering that prayer. I have seen my son make wise decision after wise decision when it comes to the moral issues of life. He doesn't drink alcohol, doesn't use drugs, and wants to stay sexually pure until marriage. For example, he is a sophomore in college and has met a girl he is very smitten with. He is refusing to ask her to go steady with him or to plunge into a serious relationship with him until he can meet her father and get his blessing. He is not asking to marry her, just to start the process of getting to know her better. I believe he is showing wisdom and respect not only for the young lady but also for her parents as well. Likewise, I have seen my daughter exhibit maturity and wisdom far beyond her years. She hungers after God's word and seeks to make decisions that will be pleasing to her Lord.

In the end I have never prayed this prayer thinking it is a guarantee that my children will always make the correct choices. They still have free will. There is no magic pill I can give them to guarantee they will never mess up.

How do we live in a way that is pleasing to God? How can we figure out what the right decisions are? How do we know which plan is the one that will be in accord with His will and glorify Him? I believe there is only one way to accomplish this. It is to so saturate your mind and heart with God's word that He actually starts guiding your each and every step. We need to be diligent to make God's word a light unto our path.

Let's again compare God's word to the GPS system on the dashboard of your car. Just as the GPS system cannot help you to find your destination if you do not use it, the Bible cannot guide your journey of life if you do not study it. Notice, I said, we need to study the word. A five-minute daily devotional is not enough. If you were planning a trip to a place you have never been before how much would you use the GPS system? Would you just turn it on for five minutes upon leaving your house and then turn it off until you get lost? Or, would you leave it on the entire time allowing it to guide you through every turn? In a similar way we need to have God's word in our possession at all times so we can use it to guide us in everything we do. The way we take it with us everywhere is to hide it in our hearts. We need to become so accustomed to it that it naturally flows into our thinking in every facet of our lives.

You may be saying things like, "I have tried studying the Bible before but I just don't get anything out of it" or "I have read the Bible, but find it boring and irrelevant for life." I understand, because there was a time when I said those things. I believe that if you will finish reading this book you will get a glimpse of just how relevant scripture is to us today. There are several other things you can do to help make the Bible exciting and fulfilling. First off, all you need is to humbly ask God to reveal His word to you. His word is not understood apart from the teaching of the Holy Spirit. So, ask God to open up the eyes of your understanding through the Holy Spirit. Second, you need to learn how to study. There is a method of study called the inductive method. This method will show you how to interact with the scriptures in order to dig the truth out. Kay Arthur's excellent book called, *How to Study your Bible*, [3] will teach you how to study inductively. Third, you need to pray and ask God to give you a hunger for His word. Last of all you need to be willing to do your part. It takes work and time to mine the riches found in His word.

Ten years ago I was biblically illiterate and frustrated. I had trouble even reading my Bible for a few minutes a day. I was trying to develop a consistent time of morning devotions. I would open God's word and read but would soon find my mind wandering to all of the things that were before me that day. Some days I would just forget and later in the day I would remember I had not done my daily reading. Other days I would read, but I would feel like I was wasting valuable time because I did not understand anything. I felt I was not receiving anything of value.

One evening I was complaining to a friend about my frustration with God's word. She patiently listened to me rant on and on about how hard I was trying and how I felt I was getting nowhere. Then she said something to me that at first made me angry but in the end proved to be correct. She told me that maybe I was trying to do it all in my own strength rather than relying on God to reveal His word to me.

I went home and prayed to God. I told Him that if He wanted me to get anything of value out of His word then He would have to perform it because I was failing miserably. Not long after praying that prayer a friend and I attended a Women of Faith Conference. The Friday afternoon speaker was Kay Arthur. Kay used her time to present to us the inductive method of Bible study. As she started her presentation she said that many people tell her that their lives have been transformed after learning how to study this way. I prayed a silent prayer that I would become one of those people with a transformed life.

I left that conference with Kay's book, *How to Study Your Bible,* ⁴ in my hands and a renewed desire to understand God's word in my heart. I spent the next several years using Kay's book to learn how to study. It took a lot of hard work and a lot of requests to God for help, hunger, and understanding.

I did all of those things I mentioned earlier and God has opened up His word to me. He wants us to understand His word. He wants us to be enriched by His truth. If you truly seek to understand the Bible, He will reveal it to you. Today my hunger for His word is so strong that I study it for several hours every day. Once He gives you a taste, you will just want to keep on feasting. What I have discovered has indeed transformed my life!

What does this entire chapter have to do with the sovereignty of God? It has everything to do with it. God is the Lord of lords and King of kings. He alone rules over the affairs of men. His word is the judge of our lives (Hebrews 4:12). If God is sovereign over all, then doesn't it make sense to get to know Him? My prayer for you is that you will study the Bible as a way of life and be transformed just as I have been.

Questions for personal reflection

What things could you give up in your daily schedule in order to make time to study God's word?

What kinds of prayers do you pray for your children? Are they shallow prayers for things like health, wealth, and happiness, or are they meaty prayers for things like God's wisdom and knowledge of Him?

What is the basis of your decision making? Do you consider God as you make decisions or are your decisions based on the flesh?

Are you walking as the wise or the unwise?

2

How sovereign is your God ...
When nothing seems to make sense?

We have all been *there*. If you have not been *there*, just wait, you will get *there* at some point in your life. Many times we end up *there* through no fault of our own. Sometimes we are all alone *there*. Other times our loved ones are *there* right along with us. We may be *there* for a long, long time or our visit *there* may be very brief. Two things that are very hard to find *there* are peace and contentment. As a matter of fact, more often than not, turmoil and hardship seem to be the only things *there*. Most of the time we know how we got *there*, but we still ask, "why am I here?" Being *there* causes us to search for the answer to that question incessantly.

"Where is *there?*" you ask. "*There*" is that place you find yourself when nothing seems to make sense.

How sovereign is your God when nothing seems to make sense in your life? When you find yourself in circumstances beyond your control, how do you react? Do you run to the sovereign God of the universe knowing He has the ability to see you through, or do you crumble in defeat under the strain? Do you compromise your values and integrity in an attempt to change your situation, or do you stand firm knowing God will somehow use this for good because you are one of His?

A man by the name of Joseph finds himself in a strange new land where nothing seems to make sense and from where there seems to be no way out.

READ GENESIS 37 to discover how Joseph ended up in Egypt. Rotten brothers. To be sure, Joseph is well aware he is his father's favorite. Also, he probably should have just kept his dreams to himself, but does he really deserve to be sold into slavery? Couldn't his brothers have just ignored him? Jealousy can be so ugly.

READ GENESIS 39:1–6 for a little more of the story.
Joseph is in Egypt. He is a slave to an Egyptian master but Joseph is not in Egypt alone. Look at verse two. Who is with Joseph? Yes, God is right there with him and He is right there with you also if you are called by His name. It is easy for us to see that God is with Joseph because the Bible tells us so and we are looking at Joseph's situation from the outside. Joseph, however, is in the midst of the trial. Sometimes from that vantage point it can be hard to see that God is there.

The Bible says that God is present with us no matter what is going on in our lives. He will never leave us or forsake us (Hebrews 13:5). If we truly believe that truth then why don't we act like it? Could it be we really are not sure God is there? Or, are we sure He is there but we are not sure He is able to handle this crisis? We worry, we cry, we get nervous. We sit around and conjure up all of the bad things that could happen. We become a basket case. How does Joseph act? Verse three says Joseph's master sees that the Lord is with him. How can the master know this? It says the Lord is causing all things to prosper in Joseph's hand.

Apparently Joseph, despite his circumstances, is going about the normal things of life. I doubt very much that he is sitting on the ground having a pity party and God is prospering his hand. No, instead, it seems Joseph does the things he needs to do to continue in life. In fact, he is doing it so diligently others are noticing. What about you? When you are in a place where nothing makes sense, do you continue with life in such a way so those around you know God is with you?

Confession is good for the soul, and I must admit I have failed at this more than I have succeeded. Several years ago my mother-in-law started to have major health problems. Her health deteriorated to the point that she needed someone to care for her. To make matters worse, at the time she was the caregiver for my father-in-law. My husband, who is an only child, and I suddenly had two elderly parents for whom we became decision makers and caregivers. We loved his parents. This was a most difficult time in our lives as we watched death take them an inch at a time. It was a time of nursing homes and hospitals, a time of late night calls and uncertainty, and a time of anger for my mother-in-law.

As we walked through the first two years of that process I was an emotional mess. I cried my way through that period of our lives. The pain was excruciating. It seemed to me like God was a million miles away. He wasn't; He was right there with me guiding us through all that had to be done. Actually, I knew He was right there, but I refused to trust Him. I refused to put my belief into action. As a result I failed miserably at being strong for my husband, and I failed to bring the spiritual comfort to my mother-in-law that she most desperately needed. Instead of letting God's strength work through me I became weak and useless. This does not mean it is wrong to cry and feel sadness when hard things come our way. There is a difference in experiencing normal human emotions and becoming distraught because we do not trust God. If we believe God is in control of everything and He works all things together for good to those who love Him (Romans 8:28), then when the hard times hit we should be able to trust Him and have some measure of peace.

Joseph is acting out his faith. God is blessing him. Therefore, we can assume the tough times are over, right? Think again.

Read Genesis 39:7–20.

Joseph is doing well and because of his integrity he ends up in jail! Sure doesn't seem fair. If you're with him, God, then are you sleeping? Maybe God left. That could be the reason this is happening. Think again. Verse twenty-one says the Lord is with Joseph and is extending kindness to him. I wonder if Joseph is confused or possibly mad at God. Does he realize God is with him? Does he understand God is still in control?

Read Genesis 40:1–8.

Did you see it? Look again at verses six through eight. Joseph sees some prisoners looking dejected and asks them why they are so sad. Would Joseph react this way if he is not sure God is in control? After all Joseph is also in jail. Read the rest of chapter forty and also chapter forty-one.

Why is Joseph in jail? The last verse of chapter forty-one gives us the clue. All of the people of the earth come to buy grain from Joseph because of the severe famine. Joseph ends up in jail so he can interpret some dreams and end up saving many people from starvation. God takes something meant for evil in Joseph's life and uses it for the good of many. Could God save the people from this famine in some other way? Absolutely. We may never understand in this life why God does things the way He does them, but we should be able to come to the realization that God is always working and has our best in mind. The story does not end here. You will be blessed if you read the rest of the book of Genesis, but I will hit the highlights for you.

The famine is so severe the people of Canaan are affected. Canaan is where Joseph's brothers and family are living. Remember they are the scoundrels who sold Joseph into slavery at the beginning of this story. So, the brothers come to Egypt for food. Of course the person in charge of distributing the food is Joseph. The brothers do not recognize him but Joseph recognizes his brothers. Joseph does not reveal himself immediately, but after some dealings with them, he finally tells them his identity.

There are so many ways Joseph can react to this situation. He can refuse to save his brothers and let them starve to death. He can devise a plan to have them sold into slavery. He can do any number of things to pay them back and the brothers know it. Joseph does not do any of those things. Instead, he helps his family. What is Joseph's reasoning for not getting even? Is it his love for his family? Is it because he is just such a great guy? These things may be true but Joseph himself gives us the reason.

READ GENESIS 45:4–8.

What is Joseph's reason?

_____

_____

_____

_____

Joseph knows his God is in control. Joseph understands God is saving the nation of Israel through the events in his life. Joseph makes a beautiful statement in Genesis 50:20. He is talking to his brothers and he says, "And as for you, you meant evil against me, but God meant it for good in order to bring about this present result, to preserve many people alive."

What can we learn from Joseph? When circumstances come into your life that you do not understand, will you only see the bad or will you look for the good God is going to bring about? Joseph seems to understand that his God is worthy of praise despite his circumstances. What about you? Do your circumstances have to change in order for you to trust your God? In order for you to praise His holy name?

Let us reason together for a moment. If God is the sovereign God of the universe, the One who created it all, if He is truly in control of everything, then is He trustworthy? Hasn't He already proven He is trustworthy? After all, He came in the flesh and died a cruel death on a cross because of His great love for us. If He would go to that length to save your soul, I think we can trust Him to oversee the rest. Don't you?

The next time you find yourself in a situation that does not make sense, why don't you ask God to help you have the faith of Joseph? Then sit back and watch how God unfolds His marvelous plan in your life.

Questions for personal reflection

Think about a time in your life when nothing seemed to make sense. As you look back on that time, list the ways you can see how God was really in control of the situation.

In what ways do you have to change so you can have some measure of peace even when in the middle of a crisis?

What are some practical things you could do to change your thinking about your circumstances?

3

How sovereign is your God ...
When no one understands you?

It is not fun to be misunderstood. It is even worse to not be understood at all. All too often this happens to the Christian. It usually happens because of our faith. You may find yourself all alone in your Christianity. You may be the only person in your place of work, or school, or even in your family who has a personal relationship with Jesus Christ. When Christ enters your life and He truly becomes Lord over it, well, let's just say, your thought processes and actions will be different than those people around you who do not know Jesus. You have become set apart from the world. You are a holy vessel set apart for God's use.

Christ wants to be Lord, He wants to be sovereign, over one hundred percent of your life. He wants to be Lord over your time at work, over your free time, over your family time, over all the time of your life. He also wants to be Lord over your vacations, your possessions, your thoughts and desires, and your relationships. Yielding to His sovereignty is hard. We want to be in control. From the time we are toddlers we don't like being told what to do. We have this inborn motivation to be in control. We want to do what we desire, when we desire to do it, and how we desire to do it.

Have you truly let God become the Lord of one hundred

percent of your life? Are you holding anything or anyone from Him? What does a life look like that is totally led by Jesus? To the unbeliever, more often than not, a life led by Christ looks weird. The unbeliever cannot understand why you do not participate in certain activities. They also fail to see the importance of other things that take up your time. They usually cannot understand how you think. Your reasoning makes no sense to them. Why not live with your boyfriend? After all, one apartment is cheaper than two rent payments. Why not put your teenage daughter on birth control? After all, we don't want her to get pregnant at such a young age and birth control is easier than abstinence. The list goes on and on.

If you refer to yourself as a Christian, but the non-Christians around you don't seem to notice there is a difference between you and them, then you should probably do a reality check. If you name Christ as your Savior but your everyday decisions seem to be the same as the unsaved people around you then something is definitely wrong. If the activities you engage in, the language you use, and the jokes you tell are no different than the person who has never been inside the doors of a church, it is doubtful Christ is Lord of your life.

There is a man in scripture that stood virtually all alone. Actually out of the population of the entire earth there were only seven other like-minded people. Can you imagine? It is hard enough when there are only eight of you who believe in Christ in your workplace, or when you and your spouse and your children are the only saved ones in your extended family. Imagine you wake up tomorrow to discover you and seven other people are the only ones on the face of the whole planet who are righteous. Would you be able to stand firm? Could you still be strong in your convictions? Would you still be willing to be obedient to God even if you are the only one? What if God asked you to do something you know the rest of the world, every single person on the face of the planet, would not understand?

This is exactly where Noah finds himself. God looks over the face of the earth and sees the wickedness of man. What God sees is so bad that He is sorry He has ever created man. He is so grieved in His heart that He decides to destroy all men. Well, almost all men. Scripture tells us there is *one* who is righteous, and his name is Noah.

READ GENESIS 6:5–9.
God decides to destroy humanity from the face of the earth, but Noah and his family are righteous. A just God cannot destroy the righteous with the unrighteous. So, God tells Noah of His plans and instructs him to build a boat for himself, his wife, his sons and their wives, and two of every kind of animal.

READ GENESIS 6:10–7:1.
What is Noah's reaction to God's command according to Genesis 6:22?

_____

_____

_____

_____

_____

Now LOOK AT VERSE 7:1. What is happening here?

_____

_____

_____

_____

_____

Verse twenty-two of chapter six tells us that Noah obeys God. In the very next verse God tells him to enter the ark. We are left to imagine all of the details associated with ark building in a world so wicked that God plans to destroy it.

First of all, how long does it take Noah to accomplish the task at hand? This is no rowboat. We are talking about a vessel that is four hundred fifty feet long, seventy-five feet wide and forty-five feet high. It has to be built entirely by hand without the aid of power tools. Noah cannot call the local lumber yard and have the lumber delivered. Genesis 5:32 says Noah is five hundred years old when he starts to have children. In Chapter 7:6 we learn Noah is six hundred years old when the flood comes. Many theologians think Noah is building the ark most of this time.

For almost one hundred years Noah is building a boat out of obedience to God. It is very possible Noah has no idea what a flood is. Genesis 2:6 says the earth at that time is watered by a mist which rises up from the surface of the ground. Noah has never even seen rain. Yet, he is building an ark. Can you imagine what the people around Noah are thinking? They are going about the things of life completely oblivious to the impending doom (Matthew 24:38). They are eating and drinking and getting married. They are living life while Noah is building a boat on dry ground. I doubt the people just ignore Noah. We have all seen someone who dances to a different drummer. Do people just ignore that type of person? No, indeed. There will invariably be those who criticize, ridicule, and make fun of such a person. In my mind I see Noah up on deck two pounding wooden pegs into the gopher wood, and people are standing on the ground laughing and jeering. They think poor old Noah has lost his mind. Years later some of these same people may be pounding their fists on the door of this same ark as the floodwaters rise higher and higher.

The question for the Christian really comes down to, "Whom do you fear, God or man?" If you will really put that question into the proper perspective, the answer is easy. However, we tend to look at things from a visual, "what is happening now," point of view. The position we should be using is the one God uses, which is an eternal viewpoint. Matthew 10:28 says, "Do not fear those who kill the body, but are unable to kill the soul; but rather fear Him who is able to destroy both soul and body in hell."

Let's face it. Many times the reason we are reluctant to obey God is because we fear ridicule from those around us. It is not easy to be made fun of. No one likes to be ostracized. Being the joke of the town is not a desirable position to have. But, if we are really honest, whose opinion matters most? The neighbor down the street who has little power over your life or the God of the universe who created you and holds you in His hand? To be sure, the neighbor can make your life miserable. He can make living in your home feel like you are living in hell. The God of the universe, on the other hand, has the power to decide where you will live for all eternity.

This same God also decides where your neighbor will spend eternity.

Although God has this power over us, our main motivation for absolute obedience to God even in the face of adversity should not be based on a fear of God. Rather, our motivation for obedience to Him should be our love for Him. Isn't that what mothers and fathers want from their children? Don't we desire for our children to obey, not because they are afraid of the consequences if they don't, but because they love us and respect us enough to want to please us by their obedience? We have the power to make their lives uncomfortable. We can take away the car, their allowance, their time with friends, and do many other things to try to motivate them to obedience. However, a relationship built on love and trust is infinitely more rewarding than one built on fear and trepidation.

Can Jesus be trusted when we stand alone? Does he know what it feels like to be misunderstood?

READ MARK 3:20–22.
According to verse twenty, where is Jesus when this event takes place?

_____

_____

_____

_____

_____

What do the people from His own hometown say about Him in verses twenty-one and twenty-two?

_____

_____

_____

_____

_____

There you have it. Jesus does understand because He experiences it. No one else around you may understand, but you can rest knowing Jesus understands. People in His own hometown think He has lost His mind—or worse yet— is possessed by demons. He is betrayed into the hands of the men who will kill Him by a kiss from a friend. Another friend denies ever even knowing Him when times get tough. Then His Father, whom He obeys perfectly and with whom He has an intimate relationship, turns His face away (Mark 15:34). Jesus knows what it feels like to stand alone. Hebrews 4:15 says that Jesus can sympathize with our weaknesses because He was tempted in all things as we are, yet without sin. He understands how it feels to be tempted. He can sympathize with our weakness. Therefore, when we stand alone, when we need help to persevere we can draw near with confidence to His throne. There through His mercy and grace we will find the help we need (Hebrews 4:16).

The next time you are standing alone because of your faith, imagine the floodwaters rising. If Noah does not obey God and build the ark he will have to try the backstroke along with everyone else. I can imagine Noah thinking, as the floodwaters rise, that being obedient is worth it. Enduring the jeers and ridicule is not as bad as drowning.

Floodwaters will never rise again to destroy the whole earth (Genesis 9:11). Therefore you will probably not be asked to build an ark. However, if you are a Christian whose desire it is to live for Christ, then I can assure you there will be times when you will find yourself standing alone. Those around you may mock you, they may criticize and jeer, they may spread all kinds of evil rumors about you. A flood won't destroy them. However, there is one coming, riding on a white horse, and He will judge the nations (Rev. 19:11–16). When that happens, everyone, even those who ridiculed you for your faith, will bow their knees and confess with their tongues that Jesus Christ is Lord.

READ PHILIPPIANS 2:5–11.

Questions for personal reflection

What situations, if any, have you found yourself in where being obedient to God left you standing alone? How did you handle it?

In what ways would your life change if God were truly the Lord of one hundred percent of your life?

In what areas do you feel God is not trustworthy enough for you to be totally obedient to Him no matter the cost?

4

How sovereign is your God ...
When your world is spinning out of control?

Earthquakes	Murders
Famines	Tornadoes
Wars	Cancer
Kidnappings	Death
9/11	Floods
Stock Market Crash	

Just reading the words printed above is enough to depress even the most optimistic person. These words, most of all, represent things that imply the world is spinning out of control. Unfortunately, this is not an exhaustive list. We could go on and on. The words represent loss. Loss of dreams. Loss of people. Loss of life. Loss of treasured possessions. Loss of security. Many times these are things we read about in the newspaper or hear about on national news. They are things that are happening to somebody else. That is until *your* son is shipped off to Iraq, or *your* mammogram comes back abnormal. The tornadoes that were forecast elsewhere have hit here and *your* house is now a pile of rubble. *Your* wife dies. *Your* child gets cancer. *Your* spouse is in Tower Two and the date is 9/11/2001.

Tragedy strikes. It comes quickly and without warning. Many times it is not your fault and you could not have prevented it. Then the questions begin. Why? Why this? Why me? How could this be happening? How am I going to survive this? Will it ever be over? Is God still in control? If He is, do I really want this kind of a God? These are legitimate questions. Unfortunately, there are no easy answers.

What happens to your faith when tragedy strikes in your life? Are you able to stand firm, knowing you can trust God despite your circumstances? How a person reacts to tragedy speaks volumes about how they view their God. Is He truly sovereign? It is the hard times of life that test our faith.

There is a man by the name of Daniel who finds himself in a similar place. His world is definitely spinning out of control. One day he is going about the things of everyday life and the next day he finds himself in captivity and on his way to a strange new land.

READ DANIEL 1:1–7.

Here is Daniel, an Israelite living in Jerusalem, with King Jehoiakim on the throne reigning over Judah. The Israelites are God's chosen people, but they are in trouble. The king of Babylon is attacking. Let's size up this situation. Babylon is evil. The Babylonians practice every kind of imaginable sin. Many, many gods are worshipped there. Babies are sacrificed to appease their gods, and orgies are a form of worship. This evil empire is marching against Jerusalem, the city of Jehovah. The city where the one true God is worshipped and the place where God's chosen people live. What will be the outcome? This seems like a no-brainer. The God who created the universe will easily triumph over this corrupt, evil empire. After all good always triumphs over evil. Well, not exactly. The city is overrun. The temple is ransacked and the holy vessels of worship are stolen. On top of that, many of the people are taken hostage and marched to Babylon.

What happened? Why do God and His people lose? Is God not able to control the things that happen on earth? Did God just create the world and mankind on it and then turn His back? Before we try to answer these questions from our own reasoning we should take a look at the passage and see if God's word gives us any clues. Just read the first sentence of verse two again. You may be so shocked that you will need to read it one more time.

What do you learn? The verse says that the Lord gives the king of Judah into Nebuchadnezzar's hand. God gives His chosen people over to this evil empire. God gives them over. God does it. Nebuchadnezzar does not take the city by his own strength. Instead, God gives them over. God does not lose. Rather, God directs all that happens. God is in charge. God brings the Babylonians to Jerusalem.

It may seem I am repeating myself. I am. This idea that God directed the outcome is a hard concept to grasp. We do not like to say that God is in control when bad things happen. After all, God is love. Therefore He cannot be in control when evil things happen. We are left to assume that evil is somehow able to win sometimes.

Follow that thought process all the way to the end. If evil is able to win sometimes, and if God cannot stop it, then what does that say about God? In those instances God would not be all-powerful. If evil is able to triumph, then, in that moment, evil is more powerful than God. In that moment

God is not in control. I don't like that idea very much, and the Bible never teaches such a doctrine.

The doctrine the Bible does teach is that God is in control of everything at all times. Nothing happens outside of His control. Not even evil. Satan cannot do anything unless God permits him to do it (See Job 1:6–12). Now the question is not, "Is God in control?" but "Why does God permit evil?" This question is even harder to answer. The Bible shows us that God permits evil for many reasons. Sometimes the reasons are discernible and sometimes they are not. Some reasons are: to make us more holy, to grow our faith, to get our attention, to punish us for sin, and sometimes to bring a lost person to saving faith. The crux of the matter is God is God. He is in control of all things at all times. Why He does things the way He chooses to do them is not for us to figure out. As a matter of fact, we cannot figure them out because He is God and we are human.

Our time and energy would be better served by coming to the understanding that He is in control and then putting our faith into action. We need to face the difficult situations with a keen awareness that God is in control. We need to understand that although this particular thing in our life is a shock to us, it has not caught God by surprise because He knows all about it and has permitted it. Then we will be able to walk through these difficult situations without wavering in our faith, without despair, and in a way which is pleasing to the Father. This is where Daniel comes in. You should have seen in those first seven verses of Daniel chapter one that Daniel is one of the intelligent, handsome youths who is taken captive. Daniel, along with others, is to be indoctrinated in Babylonian culture and customs by attending a special school for three years.

READ DANIEL 1:5 AGAIN, THEN READ VERSES 8–13.
What is offered to these youths that are being educated according to verse five?

_____

_____

_____

_____

According to verse eight how does Daniel feel about this? What does he decide to do?

_____

_____

_____

_____

Daniel, despite his situation, is faithful to his God. He has dietary laws, which must be followed. The food from the king's table has probably been offered to idols. Also, the meat is most likely not killed and cooked in the proper Jewish way. Daniel makes up his mind not to defile himself. In what other ways could Daniel react to his circumstances? He could decide that if God is going to let him be taken captive, then forget following the rules. Isn't this what we see happening all too often? People often think this way: God says, "do not commit adultery," but this marriage is miserable and this other person fulfills me in ways my spouse never could. My boss is a mean and unreasonable person, so therefore it is okay to lie on my time sheet. After all, he steals from his customers all of the time. The excuses go on and on.

Daniel never makes excuses. There is not one time in his life where he reacts in an unfavorable way to his circumstances. You may not know Daniel's entire story but I'll bet you remember the story of Daniel in the lion's den. When Daniel is thrown into the lion's den as punishment for praying to his God, Daniel remains faithful. What you may not realize is that in chapter one when Daniel is taken captive and decides not to defile himself it is approximately 605BC. He is thrown in the lion's den during the reign of Darius sometime after 539 BC. This means he has lived in exile in a strange, evil land for sixty-five plus years and is still being faithful to his God despite his circumstances. Daniel always acts like he knows his God is in control.

I said earlier that God is in control of all things at all times. How can I be so sure of that? I can stand firmly on this belief because it is what the Bible teaches. Read the following verses and then list beside each reference what it says God is in control over.

PSALM 139:1–16

_____

_____

_____

_____

_____

JOB 38:1–41

_____

_____

_____
_____
_____

JOHN 19:10–11

_____
_____
_____
_____
_____

PSALM 103:19

_____
_____
_____
_____
_____

PSALM 47:7–8

_____
_____
_____
_____
_____

PSALM 59:13

_____
_____
_____
_____
_____

GENESIS 14:19-22

_____

_____

_____

_____

JOB 37:5–13

_____

_____

_____

_____

DANIEL 2:20–22

_____

_____

_____

_____

There are many more verses I could give to you to demonstrate God's sovereignty. However, from the ones listed above you should be getting the idea that God is ruler over all. So, what are we to think when the bad times come? When our world is spinning out of control? When tragedy strikes our life? If God is in control even in the midst of tragedy, then can we trust Him? If He has permitted this horrible situation to touch my life, can He be trusted?

READ ROMANS 8:28 AND 38–39.
When tragedy strikes, knowing God is in control will bring

you peace. Even though you may be hurting more than you think is possible, you can be at peace. Why? Because if you love God and are called according to His purpose, even the terrible tragedies will work together for your ultimate good. Nothing can separate you from the love God has for you. God sent His only Son whom He loves very much to die so you could spend eternity with Him. If God has the power to take care of eternity for you then He certainly has the power to work the tragedies for good in your life.

When 9/11 occurred many people were asking, "where is God?" They wanted to know "why?" Well, I cannot tell you why 9/11 happened, but I can definitely tell you where God was. He was on His throne, where He has been for all eternity, ruling over the affairs of men (Psalm 45:6). He will continue to sit on that same throne throughout all eternity. He is the sovereign God of the universe. The promise in Romans 8 is that He can and will work the events of 9/11 and all the other events of life for good for the Christian.

There is one person whose life has forever been changed by the events of 9/11 who understands this truth. Her name is Lisa Beamer. The date is September 11, 2001 and Lisa's husband Todd is a passenger on United Flight 93. Flight 93 is hijacked as part of the attack on this country. The passengers in that plane come to an understanding through phone calls made to loved ones that their hijackers are part of a larger terrorist plot and the plane will most likely be used as a weapon for more destruction and death. The passengers decide to fight back. They are successful in keeping the hijackers from carrying out their mission. However, in the process the plane crashes in a field in Pennsylvania, five miles from this author's home, killing all on board.

In an instant Lisa becomes a single mother of two little boys, with a baby girl on the way. In a moment her life is forever changed. Many hopes and dreams are shattered in a blink of an eye. How does a person cope in the midst of such tremendous loss? Lisa copes by turning to the One in whom she has put her trust. Lisa is a Christian and has a very real understanding that God is in control of all things. In her book *Let's Roll*[5] Lisa says, "My life since September 11 includes many human sorrows and challenges, and every day I must choose how to confront them. I can sink into depression or anger or anxiety; or I can trust that God is working everything for my good. I have chosen to believe God—to believe He loves me and has a plan now and for eternity. I don't claim to understand, but I choose daily—even moment by moment—to have faith not in what is seen, but in what is unseen. The road ahead is uncertain and even scary at times, but I believe that God will provide what's best for me, just when I need it. Even now, in the midst of great sorrow, there is much to be thankful for—a great family, wonderful friends, and a strong community of faith. I try to appreciate my blessings every day."

As I sit writing this chapter I find myself asking if I can live out what I am writing to you. I took my father to the hospital today to have a biopsy performed on his throat. That word biopsy is a scary word. When a doctor says biopsy, well, your breath just catches in your throat. My father may be perfectly fine, or in the next few weeks we may come to the realization that cancer has come into our lives. Believe me when I tell you that I have thought over all the scenarios. Most of them I do not like very well.

If the test results are bad news and my father does have cancer, how will I react? I will cry. I will hurt. I will put my knees on the floor and beg God to change things. Do those things mean I do not trust God? Does it mean God is really not in control? Absolutely not. It just means that even though God knows the outcome, I do not. It means the unknown can be scary. It means that I love my father and do not want him to suffer. I will still hold on to the facts I know to be true about my God. He is in control, even in this. He loves me and I love Him. He only has my good in mind. For these things I will forever praise Him, not just in the good times, but in those times when I hurt as well.

Questions for personal reflection

Over what is God sovereign? Is there anything He does not control?

What does trusting God in the hard times look like?

When tragedy touches your life, how do you respond?

The next time tragedy touches your life, will you respond differently than you have in the past?

5

How sovereign is your God …
When God asks you to do hard things?

In chapter one, we pondered the idea of using God's word as a guidebook for our life. We looked at the idea of trying to live life as a wise person. How does all of that fit in to the idea of being obedient to God? What if God asks us to do something that we really do not want to do?

I would like to give you a word of caution at this point. Many people will say that God has told them to do something because they want to justify their behavior. God will never ask anyone to do anything that violates the principles and commands set forth in His word.

Determining if God is speaking to you can be a very subjective thing. Many times we may *feel* like God is speaking to us, but listening to feelings alone can be very dangerous. Suppose you think that God is speaking to you and has asked you to do a specific thing. The first thing you should do is to determine if you would have to sin in order to carry out the request. If you conclude that the action will not violate any of God's principles, then the next thing you should do is pray. Ask God for confirmation. You may also choose to seek counsel from a trusted spiritual leader.

When we determine that God is asking us to do something we then have a decision to make. We need to choose whether to be obedient or disobedient. The truth of the matter is that sometimes being obedient is hard. Many times it will require us to trust God for the outcome.

In 1988 I started a home drafting & design business. I had found out that I was pregnant with our first child and desperately wanted to be a stay at home mom. My husband, Roger, and I felt strongly that we did not want to put our child into a day care situation. So, I started the business hoping that it would supplement our income just enough to allow me to stay home. God was good to us and the business grew. Before we knew it we had been in business for ten years and had ten employees. In addition my husband, Roger, had quit his full time job to come into the business.

The occurrence of 9/11 caused a drastic downturn in our business. Most of the employees were laid off over the next few years and my husband had to seek employment outside our business. This meant that I was working full time and responsible for managing the business as well as completing the production. During this time I was growing by leaps and bounds in my faith and sensed God calling me into ministry. I knew that in order to be effective in any ministry God might call me to that I would have to prepare. I shared these thoughts with my husband explaining that I would like to dismantle the business and take some Bible College courses.

Roger was hoping that business would take off again so he could come back and work in it. He agreed to the college courses but did not want to dismantle the business. I ordered my first course from Moody Bible College and the process of working almost full time and trying to complete college courses began.

Several months into this Roger came home from a men's Bible study and said we needed to talk. He told me that in the Bible study the thought that he was not being submissive to what God wanted to do in my life convicted him. With tears in his eyes he agreed to let me start dismantling the business and pursue my studies in preparation for ministry. He shared with me that this was not a decision he wanted to make but felt he had to do this in order to be obedient to God. Our sixteen-year-old daughter listened to our conversation and told me a few hours later that she wanted to marry someone just like her dad some day. What a wonderful example Roger is of being obedient even when it hurts.

What happens when we are obedient even when it hurts? Many times God asks us to give something up only to give it back to us. This is what we experienced in this situation. Six months after that tear-filled conversation we received a call. The man on the other end of the line was making us an offer too good to be true. Not only was he willing to provide us with steady work but he was willing to provide the expensive software that we needed to complete that work. God had paved the way for Roger to come back to our business while ensuring that I could continue in my studies.

What if God asked you to do something *big*? Something *hard*? Something *life threatening*? What if God is very specific about what He wants you to do, and there is certain danger at every juncture? What if it is not only dangerous for you but for your spouse and children as well? How sovereign is your God when He asks you to do hard things? Can you trust Him? What does that kind of trust look like?

I would like you to explore this idea of how much you

trust your God by completing two activities with me. It is my desire for you to really come to an understanding of whether or not you have complete trust in God. The only way I know to do that is for the ideas to become personal. It is one thing to say that you have complete trust in God in all situations, and another thing to demonstrate your trust by being obedient to God in the face of hard things.

EXERCISE ONE:

Take a moment and think of some activities that make you very fearful and then list a few below. They may be things like talking before a large group, flying on an airplane, traveling out of the country, etc. The reason for this exercise is that our fears differ. What one person finds fearful another person may scoff.

Activities I fear most:

_____

_____

_____

_____

_____

_____

_____

_____

_____

Now, with those things in mind, what if you feel God is leading you to do something for Him that involves participating in several of those things? Let's say, for instance, your most fearful activities would be the things I mentioned as examples. You are afraid of speaking before a group of more than three people, you absolutely tremble at the thought of getting on an airplane, and the thought of traveling to a foreign country is enough to make you sick to your stomach. Imagine those are your fears, and now imagine you have been asked to travel to China to give a speech to ten thousand people on a topic about which you are very knowledgeable. Your friends and colleagues are pressuring you to go, and to top it off you feel like God is urging you, if not commanding you, to go. If you don't go there may be no negative ramifications, but you feel like there is a reason God wants you to go.

Put yourself in a similar scenario using the fears you listed above. What would you do? Could you trust God to help you overcome and handle your fears or would you crumble under the fear and seek desperately for a way out of the situation?

EXERCISE TWO:

Take a moment and list some things below that if they were taken away from you the result would be extreme unhappiness or despair for you. They may be tangible things, like possessions, your retirement fund, or a person, or intangible things like a relationship, a job, or a hobby. They most likely will be things that make your life worth living or things that give you security.

Items I don't want taken away:

_____

_____

_____

_____

_____

_____

_____

_____

_____

Now, with the things you listed above in your mind, think about how you would react if God specifically asked you to give up some of those things. Notice I asked you to list things you would not want to be *taken away* from you and now God is not taking them from you, but He is asking you to *give them up*. Would you hold onto them with a clenched fist or would you open your hand trusting God to know what is best?

Of course the response which pleases God is one of obedience and trust. How radical is that? What does that kind of trust look like? Again, we have a hero of the faith who demonstrates very well this kind of obedience and trust. He obeys God even when it doesn't make any sense. You see God has made some very specific promises to him, but now God is asking him to do something that will, in essence, make the realization of those promises impossible.

READ GENESIS 12:1–4.

List the things God promises Abram in the above passage.

_____

_____

_____

_____

_____

READ GENESIS 13:14–18.

Again, list the things God promises Abram in these verses.

_____

_____

_____

_____

_____

READ GENESIS 15:1–6.

One last time, please list the things God promises Abram.

_____

_____

_____

_____

God promises Abram many things among which are land, many descendants, a great nation, blessings, and an heir from his own body - even though at this point, Abram has no children. Genesis 12:4 tells us that when God comes to Abram and asks him to journey to a new land Abram is seventy-five years old. Years have passed since that visit from God and still there is no descendant. How can these promises from God come true if this heir through whom the nation is to come is never born? Sarai, Abram's wife, has a plan.

READ GENESIS 16:1–4.

The story goes on to tell us that Hagar delivers a baby boy and Abram names the boy Ishmael. Abram is eighty-six years old when Ishmael is born. This means eleven years have passed since God asked Abram to journey to a new land. Abram now has an heir that has come from his own flesh. However, Ishmael is *not* the heir that God has promised.

Read Genesis 17:1–8 & 15–21.

Sarah does conceive and Isaac is born when Abraham is one hundred years old. The heir is finally born. Now Abraham can be the father of many nations just as God has promised. Isaac just needs to grow up, get married, and start having children. Then eventually the descendants will be as numerous as the grains of sand on the seashore. But first, before all of that can happen, God asks Abraham to do a really hard thing. God asks him to do something that does not make any sense. If Abraham obeys, Isaac dies and the promise of many descendants will not be realized. Has God lied? Maybe God has just forgotten the promise.

Read Genesis 22:1–14.

God asks Abraham to sacrifice Isaac. Isaac, the one the promises were made through. Isaac, the one who is to give Abraham all of the descendants. Abraham does not even seem to question this. He rises up the next morning with Isaac and heads for the place of sacrifice. What is he thinking?

Read Hebrews 11:17–19.

What great trust Abraham demonstrates. He understands the sovereignty of God. He knows what God has promised. He also knows God is faithful. So, Abraham is willing to be obedient, believing that God will need to raise Isaac from the dead so He can fulfill His promises. Can you imagine what Abraham is feeling? He has waited twenty-five years for Isaac to be born. He is over one hundred years old. Isaac is the one who is supposed to give Abraham the descendants. Then God says sacrifice him. None of it makes sense. However, Abraham obeys and God proves He can be trusted.

Go back and look at the lists you made of things you are afraid of and things you would not want taken from you. Again, imagine God asking you to do hard things based on those lists. Will you be willing to trust Him?

Like Abraham, God was willing to give up His only Son. Only when Jesus died on the cross, He was actually the substitution for you. We all deserve death because of our sin, but God gave His only Son as your substitution, to pay the penalty you owe. God has always demonstrated that He can be trusted. Are you willing to trust Him? Can you answer "yes" to whatever He asks? This is not an easy thing. As a matter of fact it is so hard we cannot do it in our own strength. In light of that fact please take a few moments right now and pray to your heavenly Father. Ask Him to increase your faith. Ask Him to empower you to trust Him fully.

Maybe you are reading this book and you have never trusted Christ with your own life. Maybe you have not made Christ your savior. He is trustworthy, my friend. If you trust Him as your savior He will make your life new. Then at the end of your earthly life He will take you to be with Him forever in a beautiful place called heaven. All you need to do is simply go to Him in prayer. Tell Him you want Him to save you from your sins and you want to trust Him with your life. If you pray that prayer, please let me know so I may praise God for your salvation!

Questions for personal reflection

List the things you are not willing to give to God.

List the things you are hesitant to do for God.

What things can you start doing today that would help you to totally trust God?

6

How sovereign is your God ...
When you need a miracle?

Who do you run to in time of need? Who is the first person you want to talk to when something bad touches your life? When you have great concerns and fear the worst, who is it that you call? Maybe you call your best friend or your mother. Maybe you call the doctor, the lawyer, or the psychiatrist. A better question might be: why do you call on that person?

When you have received the worst news possible and you need a miracle do you call on God first? Do you go to Him knowing you can trust Him no matter the outcome? Why is it God can prove Himself faithful again and again, but when we have problems, or even when we don't, we do not go to Him first? Many times God is our last hope. I have tried everything else and nothing has worked. Maybe I should pray. Just watch the nightly news. We as a nation have taken God out of everything, but let a 9/11 happen or a school shooting and the anchorman is talking about praying to God.

I fear that many times, instead of God being our first hope, we make Him our last hope. Instead of God being the substance of our lives, He is the safety net. What is the function of a safety net? It is there to keep us safe. It is there to catch us when we fall. When our strength fails and we fall off of the high wire the safety net will catch us. Sometimes God does function as a safety net and He does catch us when we fall, but He wants to be so much more than that. He wants to be the strength in your legs and feet that guide you step after step. He wants to be the balancing rod that keeps you from falling. He wants to be your confidence that gets you off of the platform and onto the high wire in the first place. He wants to be the point you focus on, that enables you to walk from one end of the wire to the other. He wants to be the tools you use to complete the walk across the wire.

In chapter four of this book we looked at verses of scripture that show us the things over which God is in control. What you should have seen in those verses is God is in control of everything. This means He is still in control when I contract a potentially fatal illness. He is still in control when financial ruin touches my life. He is still in control when catastrophe hits home. If He is still in control, why don't we run to Him? Why don't we trust Him?

READ ROMANS 8:28.
According to this verse, who causes all things to work together for good?

_____

_____

_____

_____

For whom do all things work together for good?

_____

_____

_____

_____

If you are a Christian and catastrophe hits your life you can know that somehow God is going to work in your situation to make it work out for your ultimate good. It will also work out for the good of all the other Christians involved. This seems like an impossibility, but with God all things are possible (Luke 1:37). The problem is, many times from our limited human vantage point we cannot see how anything is working for our good. We can only see the here and now. We can only see the things of the moment but God knows the future. God can see the end result of your trial.

God does work all things together for good for the Christian, but He does it with eternity in mind. What we need to understand is God's economy is different than ours. He does not do things only for the benefit of living in this temporal world. Rather, His thinking is for eternal purposes. I know of a pastor in our hometown who says, "God's answer is always yes or better." When we pray for a miracle and God seems to say "no," it is because He can see the end result and He has something better for us.

I have a friend by the name of Anna who has managed to look at life through spiritual eyes. She and her husband Scott have chosen to see things with eternity in mind. They have chosen to trust God even when the outcome is not what they desire. Scott and Anna were married in 1999 when Anna was twenty-four and Scott was twenty-two. Like most young couples, Anna and Scott discussed plans for their future. Both of them were hoping for at least three or four children.

Their dreams started coming true when Colton was born in 2003 and then along came Susie in 2004. Life was good. As time progressed baby number three was on the way. Colton and Susie were excited to be getting a baby brother or sister.

Twenty weeks into the pregnancy Anna went for a routine doctor's appointment. This particular appointment was to be an exciting one because an ultrasound would be performed. This allows you to actually see the baby in the womb. However, something was wrong, very wrong. The doctor proceeded to tell Anna and Scott that there was no amniotic fluid around the baby. This is a very serious condition, which usually means the baby's kidneys are not functioning properly.

A more in-depth ultrasound showed one kidney had not developed and the other one was full of cysts. The doctor explained to Anna and Scott that their baby girl could live just fine in the womb but her lungs would not develop normally and once she was born she would die. Their options were to terminate the pregnancy or carry the baby to term knowing she would either be stillborn or die shortly after birth.

Anna and Scott chose to let God decide how long little Hannah Gloria's life would be and Anna carried her to term. Two days after receiving the devastating news that their little girl was sick Scott heard an almost audible voice from God, who said simply, "trust Me." Those words from God helped to sustain Scott through the months of tough times. Anna also received sustenance from God through the words of a great hymn, "Great is Thy Faithfulness." The words from that hymn which God chose to put in Anna's mind are, "Strength for today and bright hope for tomorrow."

Although God did not choose to work the ultimate miracle in this situation and heal Hannah, Scott and Anna did see many answers to prayers. They were specific prayers for the following:

- Anna's first two children had been born by cesarean section. Most doctors feel a woman should only have three or four cesareans at the most because of the danger of the uterus rupturing. If Hannah was to be delivered by cesarean then Scott and Anna may not be able to have more children. The prayer went forth for a natural delivery.

- Anna and Scott were told that Hannah would not live long but they desired to have a little time with her to cuddle and hold and love before giving her up.

- Anna's mom lives more than one thousand miles away so in order for her to be present for the birth the timing of the flight and Hannah's arrival would have to be perfect.

- Anna was also concerned with how the baby would look after birth. Many newborn babies are not very attractive and Hannah was sick. Would she look presentable enough for Colton and Susie to come and see her without getting scared?

Hannah Gloria was born by natural delivery on 7–12–2007 at 10:06 p.m. She weighed in at six pounds zero ounces and was as beautiful as a little princess. She lived for three and one half hours and was loved and adored by Anna, Scott, Colton, Susie, and Anna's mom. God had answered all of their prayers. In the midst of tragedy Anna and Scott needed some miracles. They went to their God, who is the author of miracles, and He delivered in some very special ways.

The Steltzer family shortly after Hannah's birth.

Everyone reading this book that goes by the name Christian has experienced at least one miracle. It is a miracle, which is unexplainable. It is too marvelous for words. It is the most fantastic miracle that can ever occur. Yet, we often don't think of it that way. What is this miracle? It is the miracle that the sovereign God of the universe, the One who created and sustains it all, wants to have a personal relationship with me and with you. We have nothing to offer God that would benefit Him. Yet He desires to have a personal, intimate relationship with us. He draws us to Himself, saves us from our sin, and sends His Holy Spirit to live inside of us. Because He has performed this life saving miracle in us, shouldn't that fact motivate us to run to Him first with everything that touches our lives?

The Heidelberg Catechism[6] states it this way:

Question 1: What is thy only comfort in life and death?

Answer: That I with body and soul, both in life and death, am not my own, but belong unto my faithful Savior Jesus Christ; who, with His precious blood, has fully satisfied for all my sins, and delivered me from all the power of the devil; and so preserves me that without the will of my heavenly Father, not a hair can fall from my head; yea, that all things must be subservient to my salvation, and therefore, by His Holy Spirit, He also assures me of eternal life, and makes me sincerely willing and ready, henceforth, to live unto Him.

Unfortunately, many times, what do we give Him in return? Apathy. Half-hearted service. Lukewarm worship. Grumbling and complaining. Lack of devotion. Failure to trust. We make Him last place in everything. Then all of a sudden we are in a crisis. We need some help. Sadly, even then, we many times give God last place. After all other avenues are exhausted we finally turn to the One who has not only been waiting to help, but is the only one who has the power to help.

I would like you to take a look at a group of people who see many miracles from God but are still unwilling to trust Him. The outcome is tragic. The group of people I speak of is the nation of Israel. They have been in slavery in Egypt for over four hundred years. God sends Moses to Pharaoh to say, "let my people go!" Pharaoh, however, has a hard heart. He does not want to lose his free workforce. He does not care that these people want to worship their God. It is going to take a mighty move of God to set His people free. God goes to work. He performs miracle after miracle in the land of Egypt in order to show Pharaoh and the Egyptians that He is the One in control. Finally, finally, after many plagues and the death of the first born, Pharaoh agrees to set them free. Not only do they gain their freedom but God also worked it so the Israelites leave Egypt carrying the Egyptians' possessions.

Read Exodus 12:29–36.

They flee from Egypt with God leading the way in a pillar of cloud by day and a pillar of fire by night (Ex. 13:21–22). God leads His people through the wilderness to the Red Sea. By this time Pharaoh has had a change of heart. He wants his slaves back. So, he gathers his army and all of his chariots, over six hundred of them, and pursues the Israelites to the shore of the Red Sea. The Israelites see the army coming and they cry out to God. God is faithful and provides the way of escape. God, through Moses, parts the Red Sea and the Israelites simply walk through on dry ground. The Egyptians are in hot pursuit and follow into the midst of the sea. But God looks down and causes the Egyptian army to become confused, and then God orders the waters of the sea to come back over the Egyptians. God has saved Israel and they look upon the Egyptians lying dead on the seashore.

What a miracle! The sons of Israel break out in songs of praise to God. You would think this is all they need to have unwavering faith that God can do anything. You would think that the next time they have a need for a working from God they will just go to Him in confidence knowing He is able to perform. Unfortunately, this is not what we see. The story goes on to show how these people all too quickly lose sight of all God has done. They forget the miracles He has performed in their midst. As a matter of fact, it is only three days later that they have a need, and instead of going to God they grumble and complain against Moses. God, however, is still faithful and provides the miracle they need despite their unbelief.

READ EXODUS 15:22–27.
This is the pattern for their life as we read it in the books of Exodus, Leviticus, and Numbers. They are in need many times as they march toward the Promised Land. They are in need of food, water, and clothing, the necessities to sustain life. When these needs arise, instead of trusting in God for provision they grumble and complain and talk of going back to slavery in Egypt. God provides the food, God provides the water for their thirst, God even makes sure their clothing and sandals do not wear out (Deut. 29:5). Yet, each time they lack the faith to trust Him.

Fast-forward several months. God brings them to the edge of the Promised Land. The land He had promised to Abraham hundreds of years before. God tells them to send in spies. The spies go in, twelve in number, and come back with their report. If you read the text carefully (Numbers 13 & 14) you will see that *all* of the spies agree the land is just what God said it was: flowing with milk and honey. Produce so prolific that one bunch of grapes needs to be carried on a pole by two men. No more hunger. No more thirst. No more gathering bread off of the ground. All they need to do is go in and possess it. After all God is giving it to them. But, the unbelief rises again. There are also giants in the land. We cannot go in. We will never be able to defeat these giants. We should just go back to Egypt.

However, two of the spies have learned God can be trusted. They have seen all of the miracles He has done and have come to understand that what God says, He will do. Joshua and Caleb try their best to persuade the congregation that they can't do this but God can. To no avail, unbelief wins the day. What is the result? Forty years of wandering in the wilderness. This generation never gets to enter the "rest" of the Promised Land. All except Joshua and Caleb end up dying in the wilderness.

Are Christians today any different? We know about the miracle of the cross and the empty tomb. We have experienced the miracle of a changed heart. We have seen God provide for our needs abundantly. But, when the hard times come, when we need a miracle, all too often we grumble and complain. All too often we fail to see God can make a way even when there seems to be no way. He deserves our trust.

It really does boil down to, do you trust God? Do your circumstances have to change in order for you to trust Him, or is He completely trustworthy despite your circumstances? Is God still worthy of your thanks and praise whether or not He chooses to perform the miracle you are asking for?

Three men in scripture find themselves in a difficult situation. They have the choice of denying God or becoming the king's barbecue. They have to decide if their God is worthy of their devotion even if they are killed.

READ DANIEL 3:8–15.
What question does the king ask of these three men at the end of verse fifteen?

_____

_____

_____

_____

How would you respond to that question? When you are praying for a miracle and Satan wants to know if God is capable to supply your need, how do you respond? Let's see how the three men responded to the king's question.

READ DANIEL 3:16–18.
Write out the response of the three men.

_____

_____

_____

_____

_____

These three men seem to understand that God's answer is always yes or better. They understand their God is worthy of praise despite their circumstances. They trust their God to deliver them. Their response in verses seventeen and eighteen expresses the depth of their faith. Even if God does not deliver them they will remain trusting in their God.

Basically we are talking about surrendering our will to God's will. Not only surrendering our will but also accepting whatever is God's will. Fortunately we have the ultimate example in scripture of what this looks like.

READ LUKE 22:39–44.
This passage takes place on the night of Jesus' arrest. Over the course of the next few hours He will be betrayed by a friend, severely beaten, and then hung on a cross to die a very cruel death. Jesus would rather that God would find some other way to accomplish His great plan. He wants to

avoid this situation so much that verse forty-four says He is sweating drops of blood. Yet, what does He pray in verse forty-two? Not My will, but Thine be done. What happens in verse forty-three?

_____

_____

_____

_____

Jesus has given us a pattern for how we should react when we need a miracle. I found myself in a situation recently where a miracle was needed. I had gone for my yearly mammogram and several days later received a phone call. It was the radiology department calling to say they had found an abnormality in the pictures and wanted me to come in for another series of pictures.

This situation was very unsettling to me. The thoughts of chemo, mastectomies, and extreme sickness flooded my mind. With all of my being I did not want to have to walk down that road. I did, however, want to handle this situation in a way that was pleasing to God. I made a decision to trust God no matter the outcome and found myself praying prayers that were very similar to the way Jesus prayed that night in the garden. I told God that I did not want to have breast cancer and I asked Him to take it away if it was in my body. I also told Him that if He needed me to have breast cancer in order to accomplish something in my life or in the life of someone else then to not heal it but give me the grace to handle it in a way that would glorify Him. Basically I was saying not my will but yours, O Lord. It turned out that the second set of pictures proved negative, for which I praised God.

However, I experienced a growth in my faith from praying the way that I did. I believe that growth would have sustained me even if the results had been different. When we are willing to submit to God's will, however hard it is, He will strengthen us for the task He has brought before us (2 Cor. 12:9).

Please take some time to examine your life. Ask yourself, do I really submit to God's will or do I fight Him and demand things happen my way? Do I really believe God is in control of all things at all times and do I trust Him? Then go to Him in prayer and ask Him to increase your faith and to help you to truly submit to Him in all situations.

Questions for personal reflection

List at least one miracle you have seen God perform in your life.

As a result of the miracles you have listed how was your life changed?

Think about a time in your life when God's answers to your prayers were not what you wanted. Looking back on that time explain how God was still working.

How do you feel about the statement, "God's answer is always yes or better?"

Great Is Thy Faithfulness

Verse 1: Great is Thy faithfulness, O God my father! There is no shadow of turning with Thee; Thou changest not, Thy compassions, they fail not: As thou hast been Thou forever wilt be.

Chorus: Great is Thy faithfulness, Great is Thy faithfulness, Morning by morning new mercies I see: All I have needed Thy hand hath provided Great is Thy faithfulness, Lord unto me!

Verse 2: Summer and winter, and springtime and harvest, Sun, moon and stars in their courses above, Join with all nature in manifold witness To Thy great faithfulness, mercy and love.

Verse 3: Pardon for sin and a peace that endureth. Thine own dear presence to cheer and to guide, Strength for today and bright hope for tomorrow Blessings all mine, with ten thousand beside!

7

How sovereign is your God ...
When others are out to get you?

In chapter three we looked at the impact of the sovereignty of God when we are misunderstood by those around us. We explored how a personal relationship with Jesus makes us think and act differently than those who are not Christians.

Now I would like to take this idea one step further. What if those around us, who don't understand us, not only ridicule us but are actually out to get us? What if they are trying to bring harm to us? Should we change the way we think or act in order to avert harm? Come on, you say, we live in the USA. We have freedom of religion. No one is going to harm us for our Christianity. Oh really? How about the stab-you-in-the-back coworker who would like nothing better than to see the goody two-shoes Christian get fired? What about the two-faced person from your neighborhood who is just looking for a reason to ruin your reputation? What about your teenage child's schoolmates who would love nothing more than for the Christian kid to get drunk or high? These are all forms of persecution.

So, again I ask you. Should we change the way we act or think to avert harm? Should we hide who we are? Maybe we should just quit wearing our Christianity for all to see. We could become closet Christians. We can put the

Christian clothes on for Sunday morning worship and perhaps Wednesday night. The rest of the week we can wear our secular garb. What is the harm in doing that? After all, we are still Christians and we must protect ourselves.

Once again there is a hero of the faith who deals with the same problem. Others are out to get him. They even devise a clever plan to accomplish their desire. This particular hero's name is Daniel. Does Daniel change his actions? Does he give in to their threats or does he stand firm?

As you may remember, Daniel is taken captive by King Nebuchadnezzar and transported from Israel to Babylon. Fast forward sixty-plus years. The Medes have taken over the kingdom and Darius is now king.

READ DANIEL 6:1–5.

The other two commissioners, as well as the 120 governors are jealous. They must put a stop to Daniel's success. This should be easy to do. All they need is some type of accusation to bring against him. They need to find something he has done wrong or a time when he has completed slipshod work. Maybe they could just shine some light on an area of corruption in his governmental affairs. Try as they might, they are not able to find anything. Everything Daniel does, he does with integrity, and no corruption can be found in him.

Wouldn't it be great if it were impossible to find corruption in our governmental officials today? Just think how different everyday life would be if those in charge were men and women of integrity.

If you are a Christian then you should be striving to live a life of integrity. If someone were to examine your life would they be able to say there is no evidence for corruption or negligence found in you? Would they be forced to attack you in the area of your faith because they could find no other ground of accusation? If you call yourself Christian then you should be striving to be like Daniel. Actually, you should be striving to be like Jesus, but Daniel's example helps us to see what it looks like in everyday life.

Jealous people don't usually give up easily, and these men are no exception. In case you are thinking you are safe from attack if there is no ground of accusation to find, think again. You may always act with integrity, but evil men act with deceit.

READ DANIEL 6:6–9.
Look at verse seven. What is the first thing these men say? They say to the king, "all the commissioners have consulted together." Is this really true? Daniel is a commissioner and we can be quite certain he was not consulted in this matter. When evil men are out to get you they will use whatever means possible to accomplish their purposes. King Darius likes their proposition so he signs the injunction. What does this have to do with Daniel?

READ DANIEL 6:10.
Daniel knows what the document says and he knows it is signed. In light of that knowledge does he change his behavior? I look at this story and I tend to ask why Daniel does not hide when he prays. I mean, he can continue to pray three times every day and he can have prayer anywhere. If he knows about the injunction then why not go into his closet where no one can see and pray? Read the following scripture for more insight.

READ 2 CHRONICLES 6:18–21.

Daniel does not hide to pray because, very simply, he is praying to God. The Jewish people believe God's presence is in the temple. They are taught to pray toward God's presence. Daniel does this three times a day, every day. This is why his enemies are able to catch him. Daniel is consistent. He does not hide to pray because communing with his God is more important to him than life itself. Also, what would Daniel be communicating to these evil men if he hides to pray? Wouldn't he in effect be saying that His God is not worthy of devotion in difficult times?

READ DANIEL 6:11–18.

Daniel is caught. He is thrown in the lion's den. Even King Darius cannot do a thing to save Daniel from this fate. Look at verse sixteen again to see what Darius says to Daniel.

This simple statement to Daniel speaks volumes about Daniel's faith. First of all Darius realizes that Daniel *constantly* serves his God. I wonder how many of us have coworkers, people in authority, or acquaintances that would say they know we *constantly* serve our God. After all, Darius is not a relative or a best friend; he is the king and Daniel's boss. I highly doubt Darius knows Daniel intimately. However, Daniel lives his life in such a way that those he comes in contact with know he serves his God. Secondly, Darius also seems to realize that Daniel's God is worth serving because he states that this God can rescue Daniel.

READ DANIEL 6:19–24.

According to verse twenty-two why is Daniel still alive?

_____

_____

_____

_____

_____

Does this experience have any effect on anybody else besides
Daniel and the ones who tried to have him killed?

READ DANIEL 6:25–27.
What effect does this experience have on King Darius? From
these passages it certainly looks like Darius has come to believe
in Daniel's God and he commands others to believe also. What
are the ramifications if Daniel decides to change his actions
because of the injunction and hides in his closet to pray?

What would be the ramifications in your life if you continued to live for Christ even when it means possible harm?
What about our nation as a whole? Many surveys reveal that
something like eighty-six percent of Americans claim to be
Christian. Why is it then that God's word has been taken
out of our schools? Why can we not pray at graduation cer-
emonies? Why is it illegal for the Ten Commandments to
be displayed on government properties? Have the Christians
in this nation really continued in their faith no matter the
circumstances? What do you think would happen if eighty-
six percent of all school students in the nation carried their
Bibles to school tomorrow?

READ MATTHEW 5:10–16

In what two ways does Jesus describe Christians in this passage?

_____

_____

_____

_____

_____

Salt is a preservative. Light illumines the darkness. In this perverse and darkened world Christians are salt and light. Our lifestyle should help to stop or slow decay and should illumine the truth about God. Whether we like it or not others are watching us. Just as all those around him were observing Daniel our actions and beliefs are manifested to the unsaved in our communities.

Both metaphors of salt and light raise important questions about Christian involvement in society regarding all forms of separatism or withdrawal. We are not called to control secular power structures; neither are we promised that we can Christianize the legislation and values of the world. But we must remain active preservative agents, indeed irritants, in calling the world to heed God's standards. We dare not form isolated Christian enclaves to which the world pays no attention.[7]

Questions for personal reflection

If Daniel had died in the lion's den would he have lost? Why or why not?

Recall a time when you were afraid to show your Christianity because of how those around you might have reacted?

Name one person you know that is a "Daniel." This person is one who constantly serves his God and has no corruption or negligence to be found in him.

Would your friends and acquaintances list your name in response to the above question?

8

How sovereign is your God ...
When God says wait?

We live in an instant society. With the technological advances of today and the advent of computers, the Internet, and e-mail, our world has become significantly smaller. In a smaller world things happen faster. It was not very long ago that corresponding with a person on the other side of the U.S. was something that took days or weeks. Today, not only can we talk with someone on the other side of the U.S., we can also communicate with someone on the other side of the world, instantly, with the aid of a computer.

As a result of our ability to be able to communicate with others more quickly and easily, there are few things in life for which we need to wait. This became abundantly clear to me one day when my children were young and I was making them lunch. They decide they want a microwave ravioli meal. You probably know the kind. You pop off the metal top and replace the plastic lid before putting it into the microwave. Two minutes later you have a hot meal that is ready to be eaten. I place the meal in the microwave and hit the timer for two minutes. About 30 seconds later one of my children complains that it takes so long for lunch to get ready. I have to laugh and try to explain to them that they have no concept of time or how hard it is for some families, like those in third world countries, to provide a simple lunch for their children. However, the point really hit home with me. What are my children going to do when they really do have to wait for an extended amount of time?

Use of credit in our society has also helped to diminish the amount of time we need to wait. Our parent's generation waited to purchase things until they had saved the money required. Today if we want something we just flash the old credit card and buy it on the spot. Many of the items we consider a necessity today our parents would have considered a luxury.

In addition to the fact that we live in an instant society is the fact that we also live in a very busy society. There was a time in our history when people had front porches because they would actually sit on them and enjoy quiet and relaxing times visiting with neighbors and friends. Today most homes do not even have a front porch and even if they do, the porches are hardly ever used. Many people do not even know their next door neighbor's names. Most of us are so busy running from one activity to the next that we do not have any downtime to just relax. This busy factor also makes it hard for us to wait. We are in a hurry; we have things to accomplish and places to go; we do not have time to wait.

What happens when God says, "wait?" We need an answer to our problem and we pray, but God does not seem to be answering. Could it be He is telling us to wait? We need God to intervene, so we pray, but the intervention does not come. This "thing" has been going on for too long. God may be saying, "wait." How do we respond to that? Do we become impatient and try to get God to work faster? Do we try to help God? Maybe we should just take matters into our own hands and let the chips fall where they may.

In chapter five we saw how Abraham did the hard thing and obeyed God even when all looked lost. Again, we need to look at Abraham because he was a man who needed to wait. Before Abraham was known by that name his name was Abram. We learn in Genesis seventeen that God changes his name. We see in Genesis twelve that God appears to Abram and promises to make of him a great nation and God tells Abram to leave his country for a place that God will show him.

READ GENESIS 12:4.
How old is Abram when God appears to him with these promises?

_____

_____

_____

_____

_____

Abram leaves his country and travels for some time and then God appears to him again. This time God promises Abram several things, among which is the promise of the seed and descendants as numerous as the stars of the sky. What is Abram's condition at this time as far as heirs go?

_____

_____

_____

_____

_____

READ GENESIS 15:2–4.
Abram and Sarai are childless but God has promised that one born of Abram's body will be his heir. Now, Abram and

Sarai are not getting any younger. Abram is well past the age of seventy-five years old at this point. He is probably still able to father a child but how much longer will he be able to do this? Genesis 11:30 tells us Sarai is barren. She is no longer considered to be the proper age to bear children. So, Sarai comes up with a plan. Apparently, God needs help. God has said the child will come from Abram's own body.

READ GENESIS 16:1–3.
What is Sarai's plan?

_____

_____

_____

_____

_____

READ GENESIS 16:4–6.
According to those verses would you say Sarai's plan was pleasing to God? Why or why not?

_____

_____

_____

_____

_____

In the culture of Abraham's time this type of relationship with your wife's maid was not condemned. Sarai's plan seems to be all right. After all, God did say the heir would come from Abram's own body. But, I think there is a clue here that God is not pleased with the plan. The clue to me is the fact that Hagar's pregnancy causes strife in Abram's household. Sarai becomes jealous and treats Hagar badly. Abram allows this to take place. If this were really God's plan would there really be this much sin involved?

READ GENESIS 16:16.
How old is Abram when Ishmael is born?

_____

_____

_____

_____

_____

How long had Abram waited for an heir to be born?

_____

_____

_____

_____

Some time later God appears to Abram yet again. As before God promises him an heir and many descendants.

READ GENESIS 17:1.
How old is Abram this time?

_____

_____

_____

_____

God goes on to change Abram's name to Abraham and Sarai's name to Sarah and tells them that in one year Sarah will have a son. One year later Sarah has a son and names him Isaac. Abraham is seventy-five years old when God asks him to leave Haran and at the time of Isaac's birth he is one hundred years old. Abraham has waited twenty-five years.

There are a few things we can learn from this story. First of all, when God makes a promise we can trust it. Even when there seems to be no way, God can make a way. Secondly, there will be times when God will require you to do something to make His promise to you come true. However, I feel God will make it very clear when He wants you to act. If you feel that you should help God to make the promise come true, I would suggest a time of intense prayer and Bible study to determine if that is really God's will.

There is another hero of the faith who is told to wait and in him I believe we have the proper example of how we are to act as we wait. This hero's name is David. Now, David is a man after God's own heart. David finds himself living in a beautiful house and he is troubled about this because God is dwelling in a tabernacle made of curtains. David wants to build a temple for the Lord.

READ 1 CHRONICLES 17:1–15.
What is God's reaction to David's desire to build a temple?

_____

_____

_____

_____

_____

Whom has God chosen to build the temple?

_____

_____

_____

_____

_____

READ 1CHRONICLES 17:16–27.

What is David's reaction to God's direction?

_____

_____

_____

_____

_____

READ 1CHRONICLES 22.

What do you see in these passages that give you more insight
into David's reaction to God saying, "wait?"

_____

_____

_____

_____

_____

David wants to build a temple for God. God tells David
to wait, for He wants Solomon to build the temple. David
reacts by praising God and goes about making preparations
so Solomon will be able to build when the time comes.

In what other ways could David have reacted?

_____

_____

_____

_____

_____

We have seen two heroes from the Old Testament. Both are told to wait. One waits with praise and adoration and obedience. The other jumps ahead and tries to solve the problem in his own strength. God accomplishes His purpose in both instances but not without strife and heartache where disobedience occurs.

Before we leave this idea of waiting let's take a few minutes to discover the benefits of waiting upon the Lord. Read the following passages and then list beside each one the benefit received as a result of waiting.

PSALM 40:1–3

_____

_____

_____

_____

_____

ISAIAH 30:18 & DANIEL 12:12

_____

_____

_____

_____

_____

LAMENTATIONS 3:25

_____

_____

_____

_____

_____

PSALM 25:1–3 & ISAIAH 49:23

_____
_____
_____
_____
_____

ISAIAH 40:31

_____
_____
_____
_____
_____

PSALM 37:9

_____
_____
_____
_____
_____

PROVERBS 20:22

_____
_____
_____
_____
_____

Questions for personal reflection

Relate a time in your life when you felt God was asking you to wait.

How did you react to the waiting? Did you try to solve the problem in your own strength? If so, in what ways?

Do you feel your ability to wait on the Lord is in anyway related to how much you trust Him?

The next time God asks you to wait, in what ways will you change how you respond?

9

How sovereign is your God ...
When you have sinned?

In the preceding eight chapters we have explored the magnitude of God's sovereignty. At this point you should be coming to the conclusion that there is nothing over which God is not in control. Lest you start to think man is just a puppet dangling from the hand of God, we had better take a look at man's responsibility. What part does an individual person's choices and decisions play in God's grand scheme? Does man really have the freedom of choice if God is sovereign over all? The scriptures indicate man is both responsible and accountable for his decisions.

This is a great mystery that has perplexed many a theologian down through the ages. God has a sovereign plan and His plan will not be thwarted. He also has given man the freedom of choice. Somehow God is still able to make His plan work despite the fact that mankind does not always choose the right things. The answer to this paradox may lie in the fact that although mankind has freedom of choice, it is God who chooses the consequences we enjoy or endure as a result of those choices.

Very early in Israel's history we find God making it clear to the children of Israel that He is the one who chooses the consequences.

READ DEUTERONOMY 28.

According to these verses did the children of Israel have the freedom to choose?

_____

_____

_____

_____

Were they aware of the difference between a right and wrong choice?

_____

_____

_____

_____

Who is responsible for the consequences?

_____

_____

_____

_____

From what you know about the children of Israel down through history, did they make more good choices or more wrong choices?

_____

_____

_____

_____

_____

Many times down through the ages the children of Israel are disobedient. God always followed through with the appropriate blessing or curse in response to their actions. They are taken into captivity time and time again because of their failure to obey God. Today, we as Christians have entered into a covenant of grace with our God. We are no longer under the covenant of the law. When we come to faith in Christ, God takes His law and writes it on our hearts (Hebrews 10:16). He then gives us His Holy Spirit to live inside of us and to help us make correct decisions (Eph. 1:13, 2 Peter 1:2–4). Unfortunately, the old sin nature is still alive and well. Many times we find ourselves in a war between what the flesh wants to do and what the Holy Spirit wants us to do. However, God is still in control of the consequences we will face as a result of the decisions we make.

So, how sovereign is your God when you have sinned? When you have transgressed against Him and the consequences are coming, how do you react? Do you shake your fist in God's face and scream, "it is not fair?" Do you blame someone else for the consequences that you have caused? "It is my parents' fault. I had a rotten childhood." Maybe you make matters worse by committing a second wrong to try to right the first one.

How are we to react when we are in the midst of consequences as a result of our sin? I believe there is one person who has modeled well for us what our reaction should look like. Let's take another look at David. He is a great king who commits a great sin and the punishment for that sin is severe.

READ 2 SAMUEL 11.

List the sins David commits.

_____

_____

_____

_____

_____

READ 2 SAMUEL 12:1–14.

Sin has a way of making one's heart hard. Does David at first recognize the great sin he has committed?

_____

_____

_____

_____

Is David still accountable for his sin even though he does not recognize it for what it is?

_____

_____

_____

_____

What are the consequences that God will bring to David as a result of his sin?

_____

_____

_____

_____

READ 2 SAMUEL 12:15–23.

According to verses fifteen through seventeen, what is David's response to God's punishment?

_____

_____

_____

_____

_____

Look at verse twenty. What does David do when he realizes God has carried out the punishment?

_____

_____

_____

_____

_____

David's actions are perplexing to his servants. What do you see in verses twenty-one through twenty-three that speak to David's understanding of God's sovereignty?

_____

_____

_____

_____

_____

I find this story fascinating. David has committed terrible crimes of lust, adultery, deception, and murder, just to name a few. With each passing sin his heart gets more hard, which is evidenced by the fact that he has to be told that he has sinned. Once he realizes just how grievously he has acted he immediately accepts the responsibility for what he has done. I find this in stark contrast to what we see happening in our world today. We are living in a society where people do not want to be held accountable for their actions. When something goes wrong, it is always someone else's fault. My parents did not raise me right; therefore, I cannot help it that I steal. I was on drugs at the time of the crime so obviously I was not able to think clearly. The list of excuses, the reasons to blame others, goes on and on.

Not only does David accept responsibility for his crimes but he also accepts the punishment God has chosen. To be sure he tries to get God to change His mind, but he does not rail against God. Instead, he spends time fasting and praying in total respect hoping God will change His mind.

God does not change His mind and the child dies. David's reaction to this development is probably the most fascinating part of this story to me. The child dies. David cleans himself up and goes to worship his God. David seems to understand that God is the One who decides the consequences. So, he accepts the consequences for what they are and continues his life in service to his God.

The concept that God chooses the consequences is also true when we are obedient. Unfortunately, I think we often times fail to realize this as well. Many times we find ourselves in situations that are very uncomfortable. Sometimes making the correct decision in God's eyes can be extremely difficult. Let's face it. There are times when it is far easier to sin than to be obedient. In those times I really believe God will reward mightily for obedience.

Questions for personal reflection

How do you react when you face the realization that you have sinned? Do you accept responsibility or do you try to pass the buck?

Relate a time when you chose either to be obedient or disobedient and the consequences that resulted from your decision. Share how you saw God working in the consequences.

David accepted his consequences and went to worship God. How do you react to the consequences of your decisions? Do the consequences drive you closer to God or further away?

10

How sovereign is your God ...
When good things come into your life?

Affluence, wealth, the American dream. Fame, fortune, independence. A faster car, a bigger house, longer vacations. Happy well-adjusted children, success, health.

The items listed above are basically the "good things" of life that most Americans spend their time and energy striving to gain. We work hard to get ahead in this world. We take advantage of every opportunity to move up the corporate ladder. There is no doubt about it; most of us work very hard. The raises and promotions come. We build our dream home. We vacation in the most exotic places. When we are enjoying the good things of life do we stop to praise the God who is sovereign over it all? I am afraid too many times we not only fail to praise God but instead we often praise ourselves. *I* worked hard for that promotion. Look at what *I* have accomplished.

There are many men in the Old Testament who experienced great wealth, but I want to look briefly at just two of them. One of them understands God's sovereignty and the other one has to be shown just how sovereign God is. The first man's name is Job. Job is a very wealthy man. Actually he is so wealthy that Job 1:2 says he is the greatest of all the men of the east. We also learn from verse one that Job is a blameless and upright man who fears God and turns from evil.

Chapter one of the book of Job goes on to tell us that in one single day Job loses everything he owns and all of his family with the exception of his wife. All of his possessions are either stolen or burned in three separate attacks. Then a great wind demolishes the house where all of his children have gathered for a party and the house falls in and kills them all.

READ JOB 1:20–22.
What is Job's reaction to the tragedy that has befallen him?

_____

_____

_____

_____

_____

How does Job's reaction show us his understanding of God's sovereignty?

_____

_____

_____

_____

_____

The other man whom we need to observe is named Nebuchadnezzar. You should remember from earlier chapters that Daniel was taken captive to Babylon. Nebuchadnezzar, the king of Babylon, has a dream about a great tree and Daniel is called in to interpret the dream.

READ DANIEL 4:9–27.

Write down the interpretation of the dream. Who is the tree?
Why is the tree so big? What happens to the tree and why?

_____

_____

_____

_____

_____

Look at verse twenty-six. According to this verse what is it
Nebuchadnezzar needs to learn?

_____

_____

_____

_____

_____

What is Daniel's advice to Nebuchadnezzar in verse twenty-
seven?

_____

_____

_____

_____

_____

READ DANIEL 4:29–30.

Note how much time has passed since the dream. According
to these verses do you think Nebuchadnezzar has taken
Daniel's advice?

_____

_____

_____

_____

_____

READ DANIEL 4:31–37.
Notice in verse thirty-one how quickly God acts.

_____

_____

_____

_____

As a result of his experience, list all of the things Nebuchadnezzar learns about God as stated in verses 34–37.

_____

_____

_____

_____

According to verse thirty-seven, what is God able to do to those who are full of pride?

_____

_____

_____

_____

When we enjoy the good things in life and fail to give God praise and recognition would you not say that is a matter of pride? We may work hard to accomplish, but we need to realize where the ability to work hard comes from. We need to understand who it is that is granting us opportunities.

READ JAMES 1:16–17.

According to these verses where do all good and perfect gifts come from?

_____

_____

_____

_____

According to verse sixteen, what is happening to us when we fail to recognize that God is the source of all that is good?

_____

_____

_____

_____

You may wish to make the argument that you have seen evil people enjoy good things. You may have even seen really good people endure hardship after hardship. If this happens, then is God still in control? If evil people can enjoy the good things of life how does that speak to God's sovereignty?

READ MATTHEW 5:45.

According to this verse what happens for both the good and the evil?

_____

_____

_____

_____

_____

Both the good and the evil person experience good things from God. Scripture is clear that God is in control of the good that comes our way. But scripture is also equally clear that someday the evil person will also experience God's never-ending wrath. As well, the righteous person will experience the ultimate goodness of God for all eternity (Matthew 25:31–46).

If it is true that the righteous person enjoys God's eternal goodness, and the evil person enjoys eternal wrath from God, then how do we make sure we are counted among the righteous? Are you a righteous person? Can you unequivocally say that your eternal home is in heaven? If you answered "yes" to this last question, then I would ask you what is your basis for answering "yes?" There really is only one correct answer. There is only one way to heaven.

Read Matthew 7:13–14.
According to these verses is it easier to follow the path that leads to destruction or the path that leads to life?

_____

_____

_____

_____

_____

How many follow the path of life?

_____

_____

_____

_____

_____

The Bible is God's Word of Truth. It is the authority on all of life and it does tell us how we can follow the narrow path and enter through the narrow gate. If you are following another path than the one the Bible sets forth, then you are following the path that leads to destruction no matter how sure you are that you are correct.

I have asked a lot of people if they think they are going to heaven. The majority of them answer in the affirmative. Then I ask how they know they will be in heaven. Or I ask them what basis they have for thinking they are going to heaven. Most of them will tell me they have lived a good life, they attend church, and they try to help others. Is this what the scriptures teach? Do we really get to heaven *because* we are "good" people and we go to church?

READ ROMANS 3:10–12 & 23.
According to these verses, is there anyone who is able to live a life that is good enough to earn the right of going to heaven?

_____

_____

_____

_____

_____

If we are not able to earn our way into heaven, if we are not able to be good enough to get there, then how do we enter? The scriptures say there is a narrow gate that few will enter. How do they enter? What is the price that needs to be paid and how do we pay it?

Romans 3:23 says all have sinned and fallen short of God's

glory. There is an example in the Old Testament of a group of Israelites who sinned and were under God's wrath. But God, being rich in mercy, also provided a way of escape.

READ NUMBERS 21:4–9.
What happened as a result of the people's sin?

_____

_____

_____

_____

If a serpent bit someone what did he need to do to live?

_____

_____

_____

_____

Romans chapter three tells us we have all sinned and fallen short of God's glory. We have all suffered the bite from the serpent. Is there someone or something we can look to so we can live?

READ JOHN 3:14–15.
Who can we look to so we can live and walk through the narrow gate?

_____

_____

_____

_____

Jesus Christ was lifted up on a cross and died the cruel death of crucifixion so you and I could look to Him in belief and thereby enter the narrow gate that leads to eternal life. God is a Holy God and sin cannot live in the presence of His holiness. Therefore, our sins need to be eradicated by a perfect, sinless sacrifice. Jesus came to earth and lived a sinless life so He could pay the price for our sin and give us eternal life.

READ 2 CORINTHIANS 5:21.
When Jesus died on the cross what exchange took place?

_____

_____

_____

_____

_____

When we come to belief in Jesus there is an exchange that takes place. He applies our sin to His death and thereby pays the penalty for it. He then gives us His righteousness because only the righteous will enter the narrow gate.

I want to clarify what it means to believe in Jesus. It is not an easy "believism." It is not just saying you believe Jesus died on a cross. It is exchanging your sin for His righteousness. It is asking Him to come and live inside of you and to be the guide of your life. It is realizing He is the "good thing" of life.

There is a saying you have probably heard that goes, "he who dies with the most toys wins." This saying is totally wrong because he who dies with the most toys, simply dies. He will then experience either eternal punishment or eternal life with God (Matthew 25:31–46). As another saying goes, "I have never seen a hearse towing a U-Haul."

This chapter is entitled "How sovereign is your God when good things come into your life?" We all need to recognize the "good" things we enjoy in life on this earth are from God. But, more importantly, we need to believe in Jesus Christ so God can give us the ultimate good thing, which is a great life led by the Holy Spirit now, and an eternal life spent in heaven enjoying Him forever!

Questions for personal reflection

Relate some times in your life when good things have come your way. Did you at first thank God for them or did you consider them a result of your own merit?

Read Luke 17:11–19. Which character in this story most relates to you?

Have you accepted the ultimate good gift from God of eternal life?

If you have not accepted God's precious gift of a personal relationship with Jesus Christ, please do so even right now by praying to God and asking Jesus to come into your heart. Then share this step with a Christian friend or a pastor.

If you already have the ultimate good gift of eternal life then please spend some time on your knees right now. Thank God for this indescribable gift!

Endnotes

1   MacDonald, James (2007) "The Way of Wisdom" (page 103), Grand Rapids, Michigan, Walk in the Word

2   Wiersbe, W. W. (1997, c1992). Wiersbe's Expository Outlines on the New Testament (551). Wheaton, Ill.: Victor Books.

3   Arthur, Kay (1994) How To Study Your Bible. Eugene, Oregan: Harvest House Publishers

4   Arthur, Kay (1994) How To Study Your Bible. Eugene, Oregan: Harvest House Publishers

5   Beamer, Lisa with Ken Abraham (2002). Let's Roll. Wheaton, Illinois: Tyndale House Publishers, Inc.

6   This catechism was written by Zacharias Ursinus (1534–1583) and Caspar Olevianus (1536–1584) in Heidelberg, Germany and published in 1563 in German. It was endorsed by the Synod of Dort and embraced by Reformed Churches in many different countries. It is the custom of many churches that use it to explain it from the pulpit every Sunday afternoon, so it is divided into fifty-two sections.

7   Craig Blomberg, Matthew, electronic ed., Logos Library System; The New American Commentary (Nashville: Broadman & Holman Publishers, 2001, c1992). 103.

Appendix

◈ CHAPTER I

HEBREWS 12:1–2

[1] Therefore, since we have so great a cloud of witnesses surrounding us, let us also lay aside every encumbrance and the sin which so easily entangles us, and let us run with endurance the race that is set before us, [2] fixing our eyes on Jesus, the author and perfecter of faith, who for the joy set before Him endured the cross, despising the shame, and has sat down at the right hand of the throne of God.

JAMES 4:13–17

[13] Come now, you who say, "Today or tomorrow we will go to such and such a city, and spend a year there and engage in business and make a profit." [14] Yet you do not know what your life will be like tomorrow. You are *just* a vapor that appears for a little while and then vanishes away. [15] Instead, *you ought* to say, "If the Lord wills, we will live and also do this or that." [16] But as it is, you boast in your arrogance; all such boasting is evil. [17] Therefore, to one who knows *the* right thing to do and does not do it, to him it is sin.

I PETER 4:11

[11] Whoever speaks, *is to do so* as one who is speaking the utterances of God; whoever serves *is to do so* as one who is serving by the strength which God supplies; so that in all things

God may be glorified through Jesus Christ, to whom belongs the glory and dominion forever and ever. Amen.

LUKE 12:16–21

[16] And He told them a parable, saying, "The land of a rich man was very productive. [17] "And he began reasoning to himself, saying, 'What shall I do, since I have no place to store my crops?' [18] "Then he said, 'This is what I will do: I will tear down my barns and build larger ones, and there I will store all my grain and my goods. [19] 'And I will say to my soul, "Soul, you have many goods laid up for many years *to come;* take your ease, eat, drink *and* be merry." ' [20] "But God said to him, 'You fool! This *very* night your soul is required of you; and *now* who will own what you have prepared?' [21] "So is the man who stores up treasure for himself, and is not rich toward God."

PROVERBS 1:5

[5] A wise man will hear and increase in learning, And a man of understanding will acquire wise counsel,

PROVERBS 9:10

[10] The fear of the Lord is the beginning of wisdom, And the knowledge of the Holy One is understanding.

PROVERBS 10:19

[19] When there are many words, transgression is unavoidable, But he who restrains his lips is wise.

PROVERBS 11:2

[2] When pride comes, then comes dishonor, But with the humble is wisdom.

PROVERBS 12:15

¹⁵ The way of a fool is right in his own eyes, But a wise man is he who listens to counsel.

PROVERBS 18:15

¹⁵ The mind of the prudent acquires knowledge, And the ear of the wise seeks knowledge.

PROVERBS 19:20

²⁰ Listen to counsel and accept discipline, That you may be wise the rest of your days.

PROVERBS 29:8

⁸ Scorners set a city aflame, But wise men turn away anger.

❧ CHAPTER 2

GENESIS 37

¹ Now Jacob lived in the land where his father had sojourned, in the land of Canaan. ² These are *the records of* the generations of Jacob. Joseph, when seventeen years of age, was pasturing the flock with his brothers while he was *still* a youth, along with the sons of Bilhah and the sons of Zilpah, his father's wives. And Joseph brought back a bad report about them to their father. ³ Now Israel loved Joseph more than all his sons, because he was the son of his old age; and he made him a varicolored tunic. ⁴ His brothers saw that their father loved him more than all his brothers; and *so* they hated him and could not speak to him on friendly terms. ⁵ Then Joseph had a dream, and when he told it to his brothers, they hated him even more. ⁶ He said to them, "Please listen to this dream which I have had; ⁷ for behold, we were binding

sheaves in the field, and lo, my sheaf rose up and also stood erect; and behold, your sheaves gathered around and bowed down to my sheaf." ⁸ Then his brothers said to him, "Are you actually going to reign over us? Or are you really going to rule over us?" So they hated him even more for his dreams and for his words. ⁹ Now he had still another dream, and related it to his brothers, and said, "Lo, I have had still another dream; and behold, the sun and the moon and eleven stars were bowing down to me." ¹⁰ He related *it* to his father and to his brothers; and his father rebuked him and said to him, "What is this dream that you have had? Shall I and your mother and your brothers actually come to bow ourselves down before you to the ground?" ¹¹ His brothers were jealous of him, but his father kept the saying *in mind.* ¹² Then his brothers went to pasture their father's flock in Shechem. ¹³ Israel said to Joseph, "Are not your brothers pasturing *the flock* in Shechem? Come, and I will send you to them." And he said to him, "I will go." ¹⁴ Then he said to him, "Go now and see about the welfare of your brothers and the welfare of the flock, and bring word back to me." So he sent him from the valley of Hebron, and he came to Shechem. ¹⁵ A man found him, and behold, he was wandering in the field; and the man asked him, "What are you looking for?" ¹⁶ He said, "I am looking for my brothers; please tell me where they are pasturing *the flock.*" ¹⁷ Then the man said, "They have moved from here; for I heard *them* say, 'Let us go to Dothan.'" So Joseph went after his brothers and found them at Dothan. ¹⁸ When they saw him from a distance and before he came close to them, they plotted against him to put him to death. ¹⁹ They said to one another, "Here comes this dreamer! ²⁰ "Now then, come and let us kill him and throw him into one of the pits; and we will say, 'A wild beast devoured him.' Then let us see what will become of his dreams!" [21] But Reuben heard *this* and rescued him out of their hands and said, "Let us not take his life." [22] Reuben further said to them, "Shed no blood. Throw him into this pit that is in the wilderness, but do not lay hands on him"—that he might rescue him out of their hands, to restore him to his father. [23] So it came about, when Joseph reached his brothers, that they stripped Joseph of his tunic, the varicolored tunic that was on him; [24] and they took him and threw him into the pit. Now the pit was empty, without any water in it. [25] Then they sat down to eat a meal. And as they raised their eyes and looked, behold, a caravan of Ishmaelites was coming from Gilead, with their camels bearing aromatic gum and balm and myrrh, on their way to bring *them* down to Egypt. [26] Judah said to his brothers, "What profit is it for us to kill our brother and cover up his blood? [27] "Come and let us sell him to the Ishmaelites and not lay our hands on him, for he is our brother, our *own* flesh." And his brothers listened *to him.* [28] Then some Midianite traders passed by, so they pulled *him* up and lifted Joseph out of the pit, and sold him to the Ishmaelites for twenty *shekels* of silver. Thus they brought Joseph into Egypt. [29] Now Reuben returned to the pit, and behold, Joseph was not in the pit; so he tore his garments. [30] He returned to his brothers and said, "The boy is not *there;* as for me, where am I to go?" [31] So they took Joseph's tunic, and slaughtered a male goat and dipped the tunic in the blood; [32] and they sent the varicolored tunic and brought it to their father and said, "We found this; please examine *it* to *see* whether it is your son's tunic or not." [33] Then he examined it and said, "It is my son's tunic. A wild beast has devoured him; Joseph has surely been torn to pieces!" [34] So Jacob tore his clothes, and put sackcloth on his loins and mourned for his son many days. [35] Then all his sons and all his daughters arose to comfort him, but he refused to be comforted. And he said, "Surely I will go down to Sheol in mourning for my son." So his father wept for him. [36] Meanwhile, the Midianites sold him in Egypt to Potiphar, Pharaoh's officer, the captain of the bodyguard.

GENESIS 39:1–6

[1] Now Joseph had been taken down to Egypt; and Potiphar, an Egyptian officer of Pharaoh, the captain of the bodyguard, bought him from the Ishmaelites, who had taken him down there. [2] The Lord was with Joseph, so he became a successful man. And he was in the house of his master, the Egyptian. [3] Now his master saw that the Lord was with him and *how* the Lord caused all that he did to prosper in his hand. [4] So Joseph found favor in his sight and became his personal servant; and he made him overseer over his house, and all that he owned he put in his charge. [5] It came about that from the time he made him overseer in his house and over all that he owned, the Lord blessed the Egyptian's house on account of Joseph; thus the Lord's blessing was upon all that he owned, in the house and in the field. [6] So he left everything he owned in Joseph's charge; and with him *there* he did not concern himself with anything except the food which he ate. Now Joseph was handsome in form and appearance.

GENESIS 39:7–20

[7] It came about after these events that his master's wife looked with desire at Joseph, and she said, "Lie with me." [8] But he

refused and said to his master's wife, "Behold, with me *here*, my master does not concern himself with anything in the house, and he has put all that he owns in my charge. ⁹ "There is no one greater in this house than I, and he has withheld nothing from me except you, because you are his wife. How then could I do this great evil and sin against God?" ¹⁰ As she spoke to Joseph day after day, he did not listen to her to lie beside her *or* be with her. ¹¹ Now it happened one day that he went into the house to do his work, and none of the men of the household was there inside. ¹² She caught him by his garment, saying, "Lie with me!" And he left his garment in her hand and fled, and went outside. ¹³ When she saw that he had left his garment in her hand and had fled outside, ¹⁴ she called to the men of her household and said to them, "See, he has brought in a Hebrew to us to make sport of us; he came in to me to lie with me, and I screamed. ¹⁵ "When he heard that I raised my voice and screamed, he left his garment beside me and fled and went outside." ¹⁶ So she left his garment beside her until his master came home. ¹⁷ Then she spoke to him with these words, "The Hebrew slave, whom you brought to us, came in to me to make sport of me; ¹⁸ and as I raised my voice and screamed, he left his garment beside me and fled outside." ¹⁹ Now when his master heard the words of his wife, which she spoke to him, saying, "This is what your slave did to me," his anger burned. ²⁰ So Joseph's master took him and put him into the jail, the place where the king's prisoners were confined; and he was there in the jail.

GENESIS 40:1–8

¹ Then it came about after these things, the cupbearer and the baker for the king of Egypt offended their lord, the king of

Egypt. [2] Pharaoh was furious with his two officials, the chief cupbearer and the chief baker. [3] So he put them in confinement in the house of the captain of the bodyguard, in the jail, the *same* place where Joseph was imprisoned. [4] The captain of the bodyguard put Joseph in charge of them, and he took care of them; and they were in confinement for some time. [5] Then the cupbearer and the baker for the king of Egypt, who were confined in jail, both had a dream the same night, each man with his *own* dream *and* each dream with its *own* interpretation. [6] When Joseph came to them in the morning and observed them, behold, they were dejected. [7] He asked Pharaoh's officials who were with him in confinement in his master's house, "Why are your faces so sad today?" [8] Then they said to him, "We have had a dream and there is no one to interpret it." Then Joseph said to them, "Do not interpretations belong to God? Tell *it* to me, please."

GENESIS 40:9–41:57

[9] So the chief cupbearer told his dream to Joseph, and said to him, "In my dream, behold, *there was* a vine in front of me; [10] and on the vine *were* three branches. And as it was budding, its blossoms came out, *and* its clusters produced ripe grapes. [11] "Now Pharaoh's cup was in my hand; so I took the grapes and squeezed them into Pharaoh's cup, and I put the cup into Pharaoh's hand." [12] Then Joseph said to him, "This is the interpretation of it: the three branches are three days; [13] within three more days Pharaoh will lift up your head and restore you to your office; and you will put Pharaoh's cup into his hand according to your former custom when you were his cupbearer. [14] "Only keep me in mind when it goes well with

you, and please do me a kindness by mentioning me to Pharaoh and get me out of this house. ¹⁵ "For I was in fact kidnapped from the land of the Hebrews, and even here I have done nothing that they should have put me into the dungeon." ¹⁶ When the chief baker saw that he had interpreted favorably, he said to Joseph, "I also *saw* in my dream, and behold, *there were* three baskets of white bread on my head; ¹⁷ and in the top basket *there were* some of all sorts of baked food for Pharaoh, and the birds were eating them out of the basket on my head." ¹⁸ Then Joseph answered and said, "This is its interpretation: the three baskets are three days; ¹⁹ within three more days Pharaoh will lift up your head from you and will hang you on a tree, and the birds will eat your flesh off you." ²⁰ Thus it came about on the third day, *which was* Pharaoh's birthday, that he made a feast for all his servants; and he lifted up the head of the chief cupbearer and the head of the chief baker among his servants. ²¹ He restored the chief cupbearer to his office, and he put the cup into Pharaoh's hand; ²² but he hanged the chief baker, just as Joseph had interpreted to them. ²³ Yet the chief cupbearer did not remember Joseph, but forgot him. ¹ Now it happened at the end of two full years that Pharaoh had a dream, and behold, he was standing by the Nile. ² And lo, from the Nile there came up seven cows, sleek and fat; and they grazed in the marsh grass. ³ Then behold, seven other cows came up after them from the Nile, ugly and gaunt, and they stood by the *other* cows on the bank of the Nile. ⁴ The ugly and gaunt cows ate up the seven sleek and fat cows. Then Pharaoh awoke. ⁵ He fell asleep and dreamed a second time; and behold, seven ears of grain came up on a single stalk, plump and good. ⁶ Then behold, seven ears, thin and scorched by the east wind, sprouted up after them. ⁷ The thin ears swallowed up the seven plump and full ears. Then Pharaoh awoke, and behold, *it was* a dream. ⁸ Now in the morning his spirit was troubled, so he sent and called for all the magicians of Egypt, and all its wise men. And Pharaoh told them his dreams, but there was no one who could interpret them to Pharaoh. ⁹ Then the chief cupbearer spoke to Pharaoh, saying, "I would make mention today of my *own* offenses. ¹⁰ "Pharaoh was furious with his servants, and he put me in confinement in the house of the captain of the bodyguard, *both* me and the chief baker. ¹¹ "We had a dream on the same night, he and I; each of us dreamed according to the interpretation of his *own* dream. ¹² "Now a Hebrew youth *was* with us there, a servant of the captain of the bodyguard, and we related *them* to him, and he interpreted our dreams for us. To each one he interpreted according to his *own* dream. ¹³ "And just as he interpreted for us, so it happened; he restored me in my office, but he hanged him." ¹⁴ Then Pharaoh sent and called for Joseph, and they hurriedly brought him out of the dungeon; and when he had shaved himself and changed his clothes, he came to Pharaoh. ¹⁵ Pharaoh said to Joseph, "I have had a dream, but no one can interpret it; and I have heard it said about you, that when you hear a dream you can interpret it." ¹⁶ Joseph then answered Pharaoh, saying, "It is not in me; God will give Pharaoh a favorable answer." ¹⁷ So Pharaoh spoke to Joseph, "In my dream, behold, I was standing on the bank of the Nile; ¹⁸ and behold, seven cows, fat and sleek came up out of the Nile, and they grazed in the marsh grass. ¹⁹ "Lo, seven other cows came up after them, poor and very ugly and gaunt, such as I had never seen for ugliness in all the land of Egypt; [20] and the lean and ugly cows ate up the first seven fat cows. [21] "Yet when they had devoured them, it could not be detected that they had devoured them, for they were just as ugly as before. Then I awoke. [22] "I saw also in my dream, and behold, seven ears, full and good, came up on a single stalk; [23] and lo, seven ears, withered, thin, *and* scorched by the east wind, sprouted up after them; [24] and the thin ears swallowed the seven good ears. Then I told it to the magicians, but there was no one who could explain it to me." [25] Now Joseph said to Pharaoh, "Pharaoh's dreams are one *and the same;* God has told to Pharaoh what He is about to do. [26] "The seven good cows are seven years; and the seven good ears are seven years; the dreams are one *and the same.* [27] "The seven lean and ugly cows that came up after them are seven years, and the seven thin ears scorched by the east wind will be seven years of famine. [28] "It is as I have spoken to Pharaoh: God has shown to Pharaoh what He is about to do. [29] "Behold, seven years of great abundance are coming in all the land of Egypt; [30] and after them seven years of famine will come, and all the abundance will be forgotten in the land of Egypt, and the famine will ravage the land. [31] "So the abundance will be unknown in the land because of that subsequent famine; for it *will be* very severe. [32] "Now as for the repeating of the dream to Pharaoh twice, *it means* that the matter is determined by God, and God will quickly bring it about. [33] "Now let Pharaoh look for a man discerning and wise, and set him over the land of Egypt. [34] "Let Pharaoh take action to appoint overseers in charge of the land, and let him exact a fifth *of the produce* of the land of Egypt in the seven years of abundance. ³⁵ "Then let them gather all the food of these good years that are coming, and store up the grain for food in the cities under Pharaoh's authority, and let them guard *it*. ³⁶ "Let the food become as a reserve for the land for the seven years of famine which will occur in the land of Egypt, so that the land will not perish during the famine." ³⁷ Now the proposal seemed good to Pharaoh and to all his servants. ³⁸ Then Pharaoh said to his servants, "Can we find a man like this, in whom is a divine spirit?" ³⁹ So Pharaoh said to Joseph, "Since God has informed you of all this, there is no one so discerning and wise as you are. ⁴⁰ "You shall be over my house, and according to your command all my people shall do homage; only in the throne I will be greater than you." ⁴¹ Pharaoh said to Joseph, "See, I have set you over all the land of Egypt." ⁴² Then Pharaoh took off his signet ring from his hand and put it on Joseph's hand, and clothed him in garments of fine linen and put the gold necklace around his neck. ⁴³ He had him ride in his second chariot; and they proclaimed before him, "Bow the knee!" And he set him over all the land of Egypt. ⁴⁴ Moreover, Pharaoh said to Joseph, "*Though* I am Pharaoh, yet without your permission no one shall raise his hand or foot in all the land of Egypt." ⁴⁵ Then Pharaoh named Joseph Zaphenath-paneah; and he gave him Asenath, the daughter of Potiphera priest of On, as his wife. And Joseph went forth over the land of Egypt. ⁴⁶ Now Joseph was thirty years old when he stood before Pharaoh, king of Egypt. And Joseph went out from the presence of Pharaoh and went through all the land of Egypt. ⁴⁷ During the seven years of plenty the land brought forth abundantly. ⁴⁸ So he gathered all the food of *these* seven years which occurred in the land of

Egypt and placed the food in the cities; he placed in every city the food from its own surrounding fields. [49] Thus Joseph stored up grain in great abundance like the sand of the sea, until he stopped measuring *it,* for it was beyond measure. [50] Now before the year of famine came, two sons were born to Joseph, whom Asenath, the daughter of Potiphera priest of On, bore to him. [51] Joseph named the firstborn Manasseh, "For," *he said,* "God has made me forget all my trouble and all my father's household." [52] He named the second Ephraim, "For," *he said,* "God has made me fruitful in the land of my affliction." [53] When the seven years of plenty which had been in the land of Egypt came to an end, [54] and the seven years of famine began to come, just as Joseph had said, then there was famine in all the lands, but in all the land of Egypt there was bread. [55] So when all the land of Egypt was famished, the people cried out to Pharaoh for bread; and Pharaoh said to all the Egyptians, "Go to Joseph; whatever he says to you, you shall do." [56] When the famine was *spread* over all the face of the earth, then Joseph opened all the storehouses, and sold to the Egyptians; and the famine was severe in the land of Egypt. [57] *The people of* all the earth came to Egypt to buy grain from Joseph, because the famine was severe in all the earth.

GENESIS 45:4–8
[4] Then Joseph said to his brothers, "Please come closer to me." And they came closer. And he said, "I am your brother Joseph, whom you sold into Egypt. [5] "Now do not be grieved or angry with yourselves, because you sold me here, for God sent me before you to preserve life. [6] "For the famine *has been* in the land these two years, and there are still five years in

which there will be neither plowing nor harvesting. ⁷ "God sent me before you to preserve for you a remnant in the earth, and to keep you alive by a great deliverance. ⁸ "Now, therefore, it was not you who sent me here, but God; and He has made me a father to Pharaoh and lord of all his household and ruler over all the land of Egypt.

☰ CHAPTER 3

GENESIS 6:5–9

⁵ Then the Lord saw that the wickedness of man was great on the earth, and that every intent of the thoughts of his heart was only evil continually. ⁶ The Lord was sorry that He had made man on the earth, and He was grieved in His heart. ⁷ The Lord said, "I will blot out man whom I have created from the face of the land, from man to animals to creeping things and to birds of the sky; for I am sorry that I have made them." ⁸ But Noah found favor in the eyes of the Lord. ⁹ These are *the records of* the generations of Noah. Noah was a righteous man, blameless in his time; Noah walked with God.

GENESIS 6:10–7:1

¹⁰ Noah became the father of three sons: Shem, Ham, and Japheth. ¹¹ Now the earth was corrupt in the sight of God, and the earth was filled with violence. ¹² God looked on the earth, and behold, it was corrupt; for all flesh had corrupted their way upon the earth. ¹³ Then God said to Noah, "The end of all flesh has come before Me; for the earth is filled with violence because of them; and behold, I am about to destroy them with the earth. ¹⁴ "Make for yourself an ark of gopher wood; you shall make the ark with rooms, and shall

cover it inside and out with pitch. ¹⁵ "This is how you shall make it: the length of the ark three hundred cubits, its breadth fifty cubits, and its height thirty cubits. ¹⁶ "You shall make a window for the ark, and finish it to a cubit from the top; and set the door of the ark in the side of it; you shall make it with lower, second, and third decks. ¹⁷ "Behold, I, even I am bringing the flood of water upon the earth, to destroy all flesh in which is the breath of life, from under heaven; everything that is on the earth shall perish. ¹⁸ "But I will establish My covenant with you; and you shall enter the ark—you and your sons and your wife, and your sons' wives with you. ¹⁹ "And of every living thing of all flesh, you shall bring two of every *kind* into the ark, to keep *them* alive with you; they shall be male and female. ²⁰ "Of the birds after their kind, and of the animals after their kind, of every creeping thing of the ground after its kind, two of every *kind* will come to you to keep *them* alive. ²¹ "As for you, take for yourself some of all food which is edible, and gather *it* to yourself; and it shall be for food for you and for them." ²² Thus Noah did; according to all that God had commanded him, so he did. ¹ Then the Lord said to Noah, "Enter the ark, you and all your household, for you *alone* I have seen *to be* righteous before Me in this time.

MARK 3:20–22

²⁰ And He came home, and the crowd gathered again, to such an extent that they could not even eat a meal. ²¹ When His own people heard *of this,* they went out to take custody of Him; for they were saying, "He has lost His senses." ²² The scribes who came down from Jerusalem were saying, "He is possessed by Beelzebul," and "He casts out the demons by the ruler of the demons."

⁵ Have this attitude in yourselves which was also in Christ Jesus, ⁶ who, although He existed in the form of God, did not regard equality with God a thing to be grasped, ⁷ but emptied Himself, taking the form of a bond-servant, *and* being made in the likeness of men. ⁸ Being found in appearance as a man, He humbled Himself by becoming obedient to the point of death, even death on a cross. ⁹ For this reason also, God highly exalted Him, and bestowed on Him the name which is above every name, ¹⁰ so that at the name of Jesus every knee will bow, of those who are in heaven and on earth and under the earth, ¹¹ and that every tongue will confess that Jesus Christ is Lord, to the glory of God the Father.

CHAPTER 4

DANIEL 1:1–7

¹ In the third year of the reign of Jehoiakim king of Judah, Nebuchadnezzar king of Babylon came to Jerusalem and besieged it. ² The Lord gave Jehoiakim king of Judah into his hand, along with some of the vessels of the house of God; and he brought them to the land of Shinar, to the house of his god, and he brought the vessels into the treasury of his god. ³ Then the king ordered Ashpenaz, the chief of his officials, to bring in some of the sons of Israel, including some of the royal family and of the nobles, ⁴ youths in whom was no defect, who were good-looking, showing intelligence in every *branch of* wisdom, endowed with understanding and discerning knowledge, and who had ability for serving in the king's court; and *he ordered him* to teach them the literature and language of the Chaldeans. ⁵ The king appointed for them a daily

ration from the king's choice food and from the wine which he drank, and *appointed* that they should be educated three years, at the end of which they were to enter the king's personal service. ⁶ Now among them from the sons of Judah were Daniel, Hananiah, Mishael and Azariah. ⁷ Then the commander of the officials assigned *new* names to them; and to Daniel he assigned *the name* Belteshazzar, to Hananiah Shadrach, to Mishael Meshach and to Azariah Abed-nego.

DANIEL 1:8–13

⁸ But Daniel made up his mind that he would not defile himself with the king's choice food or with the wine which he drank; so he sought *permission* from the commander of the officials that he might not defile himself. ⁹ Now God granted Daniel favor and compassion in the sight of the commander of the officials, ¹⁰ and the commander of the officials said to Daniel, "I am afraid of my lord the king, who has appointed your food and your drink; for why should he see your faces looking more haggard than the youths who are your own age? Then you would make me forfeit my head to the king." ¹¹ But Daniel said to the overseer whom the commander of the officials had appointed over Daniel, Hananiah, Mishael and Azariah, ¹² "Please test your servants for ten days, and let us be given some vegetables to eat and water to drink. ¹³ "Then let our appearance be observed in your presence and the appearance of the youths who are eating the king's choice food; and deal with your servants according to what you see."

PSALM 139:1–16

¹ For the choir director. A Psalm of David. O Lord, You have searched me and known *me*. ² You know when I sit down and

when I rise up; You understand my thought from afar. ³ You scrutinize my path and my lying down, And are intimately acquainted with all my ways. ⁴ Even before there is a word on my tongue, Behold, O Lord, You know it all. ⁵ You have enclosed me behind and before, And laid Your hand upon me. ⁶ *Such* knowledge is too wonderful for me; It is *too* high, I cannot attain to it. ⁷ Where can I go from Your Spirit? Or where can I flee from Your presence? ⁸ If I ascend to heaven, You are there; If I make my bed in Sheol, behold, You are there. ⁹ If I take the wings of the dawn, If I dwell in the remotest part of the sea, ¹⁰ Even there Your hand will lead me, And Your right hand will lay hold of me. ¹¹ If I say, "Surely the darkness will overwhelm me, And the light around me will be night," ¹² Even the darkness is not dark to You, And the night is as bright as the day. Darkness and light are alike *to You.* ¹³ For You formed my inward parts; You wove me in my mother's womb. ¹⁴ I will give thanks to You, for I am fearfully and wonderfully made; Wonderful are Your works, And my soul knows it very well. ¹⁵ My frame was not hidden from You, When I was made in secret, *And* skillfully wrought in the depths of the earth; ¹⁶ Your eyes have seen my unformed substance; And in Your book were all written The days that were ordained *for me,* When as yet there was not one of them.

Job 38:1–41

¹ Then the Lord answered Job out of the whirlwind and said, ² "Who is this that darkens counsel By words without knowledge? ³ "Now gird up your loins like a man, And I will ask you, and you instruct Me! ⁴ "Where were you when I laid the foundation of the earth? Tell *Me,* if you have under-

standing, ⁵ Who set its measurements? Since you know. Or who stretched the line on it? ⁶ "On what were its bases sunk? Or who laid its cornerstone, ⁷ When the morning stars sang together And all the sons of God shouted for joy? ⁸ "Or *who* enclosed the sea with doors When, bursting forth, it went out from the womb; ⁹ When I made a cloud its garment And thick darkness its swaddling band, ¹⁰ And I placed boundaries on it And set a bolt and doors, ¹¹ And I said, 'Thus far you shall come, but no farther; And here shall your proud waves stop'? ¹² "Have you ever in your life commanded the morning, *And* caused the dawn to know its place, ¹³ That it might take hold of the ends of the earth, And the wicked be shaken out of it? ¹⁴ "It is changed like clay *under* the seal; And they stand forth like a garment. ¹⁵ "From the wicked their light is withheld, And the uplifted arm is broken. ¹⁶ "Have you entered into the springs of the sea Or walked in the recesses of the deep? ¹⁷ "Have the gates of death been revealed to you, Or have you seen the gates of deep darkness? ¹⁸ "Have you understood the expanse of the earth? Tell *Me,* if you know all this. ¹⁹ "Where is the way to the dwelling of light? And darkness, where is its place, ²⁰ That you may take it to its territory And that you may discern the paths to its home? ²¹ "You know, for you were born then, And the number of your days is great! ²² "Have you entered the storehouses of the snow, Or have you seen the storehouses of the hail, ²³ Which I have reserved for the time of distress, For the day of war and battle? ²⁴ "Where is the way that the light is divided, *Or* the east wind scattered on the earth? ²⁵ "Who has cleft a channel for the flood, Or a way for the thunderbolt, ²⁶ To bring rain on a land without people, *On* a desert without a man in it, ²⁷ To satisfy the waste and desolate land And to make the seeds of grass to sprout? [28] "Has the rain a father? Or who has begotten the drops of dew? [29] "From whose womb has come the ice? And the frost of heaven, who has given it birth? [30] "Water becomes hard like stone, And the surface of the deep is imprisoned. [31] "Can you bind the chains of the Pleiades, Or loose the cords of Orion? [32] "Can you lead forth a constellation in its season, And guide the Bear with her satellites? [33] "Do you know the ordinances of the heavens, Or fix their rule over the earth? [34] "Can you lift up your voice to the clouds, So that an abundance of water will cover you? [35] "Can you send forth lightnings that they may go And say to you, 'Here we are'? [36] "Who has put wisdom in the innermost being Or given understanding to the mind? [37] "Who can count the clouds by wisdom, Or tip the water jars of the heavens, [38] When the dust hardens into a mass And the clods stick together? [39] "Can you hunt the prey for the lion, Or satisfy the appetite of the young lions, [40] When they crouch in *their* dens *And* lie in wait in *their* lair? [41] "Who prepares for the raven its nourishment When its young cry to God And wander about without food?

JOHN 19:10–11
[10] So Pilate said to Him, "You do not speak to me? Do You not know that I have authority to release You, and I have authority to crucify You?" [11] Jesus answered, "You would have no authority over Me, unless it had been given you from above; for this reason he who delivered Me to you has *the* greater sin."

PSALM 103:19
[19] The Lord has established His throne in the heavens, And His sovereignty rules over all.

Psalm 47:7–8

7 For God is the King of all the earth; Sing praises with a skillful psalm. 8 God reigns over the nations, God sits on His holy throne.

Psalm 59:13

13 Destroy *them* in wrath, destroy *them* that they may be no more; That *men* may know that God rules in Jacob To the ends of the earth. Selah.

Genesis 14:19–22

19 He blessed him and said, "Blessed be Abram of God Most High, Possessor of heaven and earth; 20 And blessed be God Most High, Who has delivered your enemies into your hand." He gave him a tenth of all. 21 The king of Sodom said to Abram, "Give the people to me and take the goods for yourself." 22 Abram said to the king of Sodom, "I have sworn to the Lord God Most High, possessor of heaven and earth,

Job 37:5–13

5 "God thunders with His voice wondrously, Doing great things which we cannot comprehend. 6 "For to the snow He says, 'Fall on the earth,' And to the downpour and the rain, 'Be strong.' 7 "He seals the hand of every man, That all men may know His work. 8 "Then the beast goes into its lair And remains in its den. 9 "Out of the south comes the storm, And out of the north the cold. 10 "From the breath of God ice is made, And the expanse of the waters is frozen. 11 "Also with moisture He loads the thick cloud; He disperses the cloud of His lightning. 12 "It changes direction, turning around by His guidance, That it may do whatever He commands it On the

face of the inhabited earth. [13] "Whether for correction, or for His world, Or for lovingkindness, He causes it to happen.

DANIEL 2:20–22

[20] Daniel said, "Let the name of God be blessed forever and ever, For wisdom and power belong to Him. [21] "It is He who changes the times and the epochs; He removes kings and establishes kings; He gives wisdom to wise men And knowledge to men of understanding. [22] "It is He who reveals the profound and hidden things; He knows what is in the darkness, And the light dwells with Him.

ROMANS 8:28

[28] And we know that God causes all things to work together for good to those who love God, to those who are called according to *His* purpose.

ROMANS 8:38–39

[38] For I am convinced that neither death, nor life, nor angels, nor principalities, nor things present, nor things to come, nor powers, [39] nor height, nor depth, nor any other created thing, will be able to separate us from the love of God, which is in Christ Jesus our Lord.

🔱 CHAPTER 5

GENESIS 12:1–4

[1] Now the Lord said to Abram, "Go forth from your country, And from your relatives And from your father's house, To the land which I will show you; [2] And I will make you a great nation, And I will bless you, And make your name great; And so you shall be a blessing; [3] And I will bless those who

bless you, And the one who curses you I will curse. And in you all the families of the earth will be blessed." ⁴ So Abram went forth as the Lord had spoken to him; and Lot went with him. Now Abram was seventy-five years old when he departed from Haran.

GENESIS 13:14–18

¹⁴ The Lord said to Abram, after Lot had separated from him, "Now lift up your eyes and look from the place where you are, northward and southward and eastward and westward; ¹⁵ for all the land which you see, I will give it to you and to your descendants forever. ¹⁶ "I will make your descendants as the dust of the earth, so that if anyone can number the dust of the earth, then your descendants can also be numbered. ¹⁷ "Arise, walk about the land through its length and breadth; for I will give it to you." ¹⁸ Then Abram moved his tent and came and dwelt by the oaks of Mamre, which are in Hebron, and there he built an altar to the Lord.

GENESIS 15:1–6

¹ After these things the word of the Lord came to Abram in a vision, saying, "Do not fear, Abram, I am a shield to you; Your reward shall be very great." ² Abram said, "O Lord God, what will You give me, since I am childless, and the heir of my house is Eliezer of Damascus?" ³ And Abram said, "Since You have given no offspring to me, one born in my house is my heir." ⁴ Then behold, the word of the Lord came to him, saying, "This man will not be your heir; but one who will come forth from your own body, he shall be your heir." ⁵ And He took him outside and said, "Now look toward the heavens, and count the stars, if you are able to count

them." And He said to him, "So shall your descendants be." [6] Then he believed in the Lord; and He reckoned it to him as righteousness.

GENESIS 16:1–4

[1] Now Sarai, Abram's wife had borne him no *children,* and she had an Egyptian maid whose name was Hagar. [2] So Sarai said to Abram, "Now behold, the Lord has prevented me from bearing *children.* Please go in to my maid; perhaps I will obtain children through her." And Abram listened to the voice of Sarai. [3] After Abram had lived ten years in the land of Canaan, Abram's wife Sarai took Hagar the Egyptian, her maid, and gave her to her husband Abram as his wife. [4] He went in to Hagar, and she conceived; and when she saw that she had conceived, her mistress was despised in her sight.

GENESIS 17:1–8

[1] Now when Abram was ninety-nine years old, the Lord appeared to Abram and said to him, "I am God Almighty; Walk before Me, and be blameless. [2] "I will establish My covenant between Me and you, And I will multiply you exceedingly." [3] Abram fell on his face, and God talked with him, saying, [4] "As for Me, behold, My covenant is with you, And you will be the father of a multitude of nations. [5] "No longer shall your name be called Abram, But your name shall be Abraham; For I will make you the father of a multitude of nations. [6] "I have made you exceedingly fruitful, and I will make nations of you, and kings will come forth from you. [7] "I will establish My covenant between Me and you and your descendants after you throughout their generations for an everlasting covenant, to be God to you and to your descen-

dants after you. [8] "I will give to you and to your descendants after you, the land of your sojournings, all the land of Canaan, for an everlasting possession; and I will be their God."

GENESIS 17:15–21

[15] Then God said to Abraham, "As for Sarai your wife, you shall not call her name Sarai, but Sarah *shall be* her name. [16] "I will bless her, and indeed I will give you a son by her. Then I will bless her, and she shall be *a mother of* nations; kings of peoples will come from her." [17] Then Abraham fell on his face and laughed, and said in his heart, "Will a child be born to a man one hundred years old? And will Sarah, who is ninety years old, bear *a child?*" [18] And Abraham said to God, "Oh that Ishmael might live before You!" [19] But God said, "No, but Sarah your wife will bear you a son, and you shall call his name Isaac; and I will establish My covenant with him for an everlasting covenant for his descendants after him. [20] "As for Ishmael, I have heard you; behold, I will bless him, and will make him fruitful and will multiply him exceedingly. He shall become the father of twelve princes, and I will make him a great nation. [21] "But My covenant I will establish with Isaac, whom Sarah will bear to you at this season next year."

GENESIS 22:1–14

[1] Now it came about after these things, that God tested Abraham, and said to him, "Abraham!" And he said, "Here I am." [2] He said, "Take now your son, your only son, whom you love, Isaac, and go to the land of Moriah, and offer him there as a burnt offering on one of the mountains of which I will tell you." [3] So Abraham rose early in the morning and saddled his donkey, and took two of his young men with him

and Isaac his son; and he split wood for the burnt offering, and arose and went to the place of which God had told him. [4] On the third day Abraham raised his eyes and saw the place from a distance. [5] Abraham said to his young men, "Stay here with the donkey, and I and the lad will go over there; and we will worship and return to you." [6] Abraham took the wood of the burnt offering and laid it on Isaac his son, and he took in his hand the fire and the knife. So the two of them walked on together. [7] Isaac spoke to Abraham his father and said, "My father!" And he said, "Here I am, my son." And he said, "Behold, the fire and the wood, but where is the lamb for the burnt offering?" [8] Abraham said, "God will provide for Himself the lamb for the burnt offering, my son." So the two of them walked on together. [9] Then they came to the place of which God had told him; and Abraham built the altar there and arranged the wood, and bound his son Isaac and laid him on the altar, on top of the wood. [10] Abraham stretched out his hand and took the knife to slay his son. [11] But the angel of the Lord called to him from heaven and said, "Abraham, Abraham!" And he said, "Here I am." [12] He said, "Do not stretch out your hand against the lad, and do nothing to him; for now I know that you fear God, since you have not withheld your son, your only son, from Me." [13] Then Abraham raised his eyes and looked, and behold, behind *him* a ram caught in the thicket by his horns; and Abraham went and took the ram and offered him up for a burnt offering in the place of his son. [14] Abraham called the name of that place The Lord Will Provide, as it is said to this day, "In the mount of the Lord it will be provided."

HEBREWS 11:17–19

¹⁷ By faith Abraham, when he was tested, offered up Isaac, and he who had received the promises was offering up his only begotten *son;* ¹⁸ *it was he* to whom it was said, "In Isaac your descendants shall be called." ¹⁹ He considered that God is able to raise *people* even from the dead, from which he also received him back as a type.

✿ CHAPTER 6

ROMANS 8:28

²⁸ And we know that God causes all things to work together for good to those who love God, to those who are called according to *His* purpose.

EXODUS 12:29–36

²⁹ Now it came about at midnight that the Lord struck all the firstborn in the land of Egypt, from the firstborn of Pharaoh who sat on his throne to the firstborn of the captive who was in the dungeon, and all the firstborn of cattle. ³⁰ Pharaoh arose in the night, he and all his servants and all the Egyptians, and there was a great cry in Egypt, for there was no home where there was not someone dead. ³¹ Then he called for Moses and Aaron at night and said, "Rise up, get out from among my people, both you and the sons of Israel; and go, worship the Lord, as you have said. ³² "Take both your flocks and your herds, as you have said, and go, and bless me also." ³³ The Egyptians urged the people, to send them out of the land in haste, for they said, "We will all be dead." ³⁴ So the people took their dough before it was leavened, *with* their kneading bowls bound up in the clothes on their shoulders.

[35] Now the sons of Israel had done according to the word of Moses, for they had requested from the Egyptians articles of silver and articles of gold, and clothing; [36] and the Lord had given the people favor in the sight of the Egyptians, so that they let them have their request. Thus they plundered the Egyptians.

Exodus 15:22–27

[22] Then Moses led Israel from the Red Sea, and they went out into the wilderness of Shur; and they went three days in the wilderness and found no water. [23] When they came to Marah, they could not drink the waters of Marah, for they were bitter; therefore it was named Marah. [24] So the people grumbled at Moses, saying, "What shall we drink?" [25] Then he cried out to the Lord, and the Lord showed him a tree; and he threw *it* into the waters, and the waters became sweet. There He made for them a statute and regulation, and there He tested them. [26] And He said, "If you will give earnest heed to the voice of the Lord your God, and do what is right in His sight, and give ear to His commandments, and keep all His statutes, I will put none of the diseases on you which I have put on the Egyptians; for I, the Lord, am your healer." [27] Then they came to Elim where there *were* twelve springs of water and seventy date palms, and they camped there beside the waters.

Daniel 3:8–15

[8] For this reason at that time certain Chaldeans came forward and brought charges against the Jews. [9] They responded and said to Nebuchadnezzar the king: "O king, live forever! [10] "You, O king, have made a decree that every man who hears the sound of the horn, flute, lyre, trigon, psaltery, and bagpipe and

all kinds of music, is to fall down and worship the golden image. [11] "But whoever does not fall down and worship shall be cast into the midst of a furnace of blazing fire. [12] "There are certain Jews whom you have appointed over the administration of the province of Babylon, *namely* Shadrach, Meshach and Abed-nego. These men, O king, have disregarded you; they do not serve your gods or worship the golden image which you have set up." [13] Then Nebuchadnezzar in rage and anger gave orders to bring Shadrach, Meshach and Abed-nego; then these men were brought before the king. [14] Nebuchadnezzar responded and said to them, "Is it true, Shadrach, Meshach and Abed-nego, that you do not serve my gods or worship the golden image that I have set up? [15] "Now if you are ready, at the moment you hear the sound of the horn, flute, lyre, trigon, psaltery and bagpipe and all kinds of music, to fall down and worship the image that I have made, *very well*. But if you do not worship, you will immediately be cast into the midst of a furnace of blazing fire; and what god is there who can deliver you out of my hands?"

DANIEL 3:16–18

[16] Shadrach, Meshach and Abed-nego replied to the king, "O Nebuchadnezzar, we do not need to give you an answer concerning this matter. [17] "If it be *so*, our God whom we serve is able to deliver us from the furnace of blazing fire; and He will deliver us out of your hand, O king. [18] "But *even* if *He does* not, let it be known to you, O king, that we are not going to serve your gods or worship the golden image that you have set up."

LUKE 22:39–44

[39] And He came out and proceeded as was His custom to the Mount of Olives; and the disciples also followed Him.

40 When He arrived at the place, He said to them, "Pray that
you may not enter into temptation." 41 And He withdrew from
them about a stone's throw, and He knelt down and *began* to
pray, 42 saying, "Father, if You are willing, remove this cup from
Me; yet not My will, but Yours be done." 43 Now an angel from
heaven appeared to Him, strengthening Him. 44 And being in
agony He was praying very fervently; and His sweat became
like drops of blood, falling down upon the ground.

Chapter 7

Daniel 6:1–5

1 It seemed good to Darius to appoint 120 satraps over the
kingdom, that they would be in charge of the whole kingdom,
2 and over them three commissioners (of whom Daniel was
one), that these satraps might be accountable to them, and
that the king might not suffer loss. 3 Then this Daniel began
distinguishing himself among the commissioners and satraps
because he possessed an extraordinary spirit, and the king
planned to appoint him over the entire kingdom. 4 Then the
commissioners and satraps began trying to find a ground of
accusation against Daniel in regard to government affairs; but
they could find no ground of accusation or *evidence of* corruption, inasmuch as he was faithful, and no negligence or corruption was *to be* found in him. 5 Then these men said, "We will
not find any ground of accusation against this Daniel unless
we find *it* against him with regard to the law of his God."

Daniel 6:6–9

6 Then these commissioners and satraps came by agreement to the king and spoke to him as follows: "King Darius, live

forever! [7] "All the commissioners of the kingdom, the prefects and the satraps, the high officials and the governors have consulted together that the king should establish a statute and enforce an injunction that anyone who makes a petition to any god or man besides you, O king, for thirty days, shall be cast into the lions' den. [8] "Now, O king, establish the injunction and sign the document so that it may not be changed, according to the law of the Medes and Persians, which may not be revoked." [9] Therefore King Darius signed the document, that is, the injunction.

DANIEL 6:10

[10] Now when Daniel knew that the document was signed, he entered his house (now in his roof chamber he had windows open toward Jerusalem); and he continued kneeling on his knees three times a day, praying and giving thanks before his God, as he had been doing previously.

2 CHRONICLES 6:18–21

[18] "But will God indeed dwell with mankind on the earth? Behold, heaven and the highest heaven cannot contain You; how much less this house which I have built. [19] "Yet have regard to the prayer of Your servant and to his supplication, O Lord my God, to listen to the cry and to the prayer which Your servant prays before You; [20] that Your eye may be open toward this house day and night, toward the place of which You have said that *You would* put Your name there, to listen to the prayer which Your servant shall pray toward this place. [21] "Listen to the supplications of Your servant and of Your people Israel when they pray toward this place; hear from Your dwelling place, from heaven; hear and forgive.

[11] Then these men came by agreement and found Daniel making petition and supplication before his God. [12] Then they approached and spoke before the king about the king's injunction, "Did you not sign an injunction that any man who makes a petition to any god or man besides you, O king, for thirty days, is to be cast into the lions' den?" The king replied, "The statement is true, according to the law of the Medes and Persians, which may not be revoked." [13] Then they answered and spoke before the king, "Daniel, who is one of the exiles from Judah, pays no attention to you, O king, or to the injunction which you signed, but keeps making his petition three times a day." [14] Then, as soon as the king heard this statement, he was deeply distressed and set *his* mind on delivering Daniel; and even until sunset he kept exerting himself to rescue him. [15] Then these men came by agreement to the king and said to the king, "Recognize, O king, that it is a law of the Medes and Persians that no injunction or statute which the king establishes may be changed." [16] Then the king gave orders, and Daniel was brought in and cast into the lions' den. The king spoke and said to Daniel, "Your God whom you constantly serve will Himself deliver you." [17] A stone was brought and laid over the mouth of the den; and the king sealed it with his own signet ring and with the signet rings of his nobles, so that nothing would be changed in regard to Daniel. [18] Then the king went off to his palace and spent the night fasting, and no entertainment was brought before him; and his sleep fled from him.

DANIEL 6:19–24

[19] Then the king arose at dawn, at the break of day, and went in haste to the lions' den. [20] When he had come near the den to Daniel, he cried out with a troubled voice. The king spoke and said to Daniel, "Daniel, servant of the living God, has your God, whom you constantly serve, been able to deliver you from the lions?" [21] Then Daniel spoke to the king, "O king, live forever! [22] "My God sent His angel and shut the lions' mouths and they have not harmed me, inasmuch as I was found innocent before Him; and also toward you, O king, I have committed no crime." [23] Then the king was very pleased and gave orders for Daniel to be taken up out of the den. So Daniel was taken up out of the den and no injury whatever was found on him, because he had trusted in his God. [24] The king then gave orders, and they brought those men who had maliciously accused Daniel, and they cast them, their children and their wives into the lions' den; and they had not reached the bottom of the den before the lions overpowered them and crushed all their bones.

DANIEL 6:25–27

[25] Then Darius the king wrote to all the peoples, nations and *men of every* language who were living in all the land: "May your peace abound! [26] "I make a decree that in all the dominion of my kingdom men are to fear and tremble before the God of Daniel; For He is the living God and enduring forever, And His kingdom is one which will not be destroyed, And His dominion *will be* forever. [27] "He delivers and rescues and performs signs and wonders In heaven and on earth, Who has *also* delivered Daniel from the power of the lions."

Matthew 5:10–16

10 "Blessed are those who have been persecuted for the sake of righteousness, for theirs is the kingdom of heaven. 11 "Blessed are you when *people* insult you and persecute you, and falsely say all kinds of evil against you because of Me. 12 "Rejoice and be glad, for your reward in heaven is great; for in the same way they persecuted the prophets who were before you. 13 "You are the salt of the earth; but if the salt has become tasteless, how can it be made salty *again?* It is no longer good for anything, except to be thrown out and trampled under foot by men. 14 "You are the light of the world. A city set on a hill cannot be hidden; 15 nor does *anyone* light a lamp and put it under a basket, but on the lampstand, and it gives light to all who are in the house. 16 "Let your light shine before men in such a way that they may see your good works, and glorify your Father who is in heaven.

Chapter 8

Genesis 12:4

4 So Abram went forth as the Lord had spoken to him; and Lot went with him. Now Abram was seventy-five years old when he departed from Haran.

Genesis 15:2–4

2 Abram said, "O Lord God, what will You give me, since I am childless, and the heir of my house is Eliezer of Damascus?" 3 And Abram said, "Since You have given no offspring to me, one born in my house is my heir." 4 Then behold, the word of the Lord came to him, saying, "This man will not be your

heir; but one who will come forth from your own body, he shall be your heir."

GENESIS 16:1–3

¹ Now Sarai, Abram's wife had borne him no *children,* and she had an Egyptian maid whose name was Hagar. ² So Sarai said to Abram, "Now behold, the Lord has prevented me from bearing *children.* Please go in to my maid; perhaps I will obtain children through her." And Abram listened to the voice of Sarai. ³ After Abram had lived ten years in the land of Canaan, Abram's wife Sarai took Hagar the Egyptian, her maid, and gave her to her husband Abram as his wife.

GENESIS 16:4–6

⁴ He went in to Hagar, and she conceived; and when she saw that she had conceived, her mistress was despised in her sight. ⁵ And Sarai said to Abram, "May the wrong done me be upon you. I gave my maid into your arms, but when she saw that she had conceived, I was despised in her sight. May the Lord judge between you and me." ⁶ But Abram said to Sarai, "Behold, your maid is in your power; do to her what is good in your sight." So Sarai treated her harshly, and she fled from her presence.

GENESIS 16:16

¹⁶ Abram was eighty-six years old when Hagar bore Ishmael to him.

GENESIS 17:1

¹ Now when Abram was ninety-nine years old, the Lord appeared to Abram and said to him, "I am God Almighty; Walk before Me, and be blameless.

¹ And it came about, when David dwelt in his house, that David said to Nathan the prophet, "Behold, I am dwelling in a house of cedar, but the ark of the covenant of the Lord is under curtains." ² Then Nathan said to David, "Do all that is in your heart, for God is with you." ³ It came about the same night that the word of God came to Nathan, saying, ⁴ "Go and tell David My servant, 'Thus says the Lord, "You shall not build a house for Me to dwell in; ⁵ for I have not dwelt in a house since the day that I brought up Israel to this day, but I have gone from tent to tent and from *one* dwelling place *to another*. ⁶ "In all places where I have walked with all Israel, have I spoken a word with any of the judges of Israel, whom I commanded to shepherd My people, saying, 'Why have you not built for Me a house of cedar?' " ' ⁷ "Now, therefore, thus shall you say to My servant David, 'Thus says the Lord of hosts, "I took you from the pasture, from following the sheep, to be leader over My people Israel. ⁸ "I have been with you wherever you have gone, and have cut off all your enemies from before you; and I will make you a name like the name of the great ones who are in the earth. ⁹ "I will appoint a place for My people Israel, and will plant them, so that they may dwell in their own place and not be moved again; and the wicked will not waste them anymore as formerly, ¹⁰ even from the day that I commanded judges *to be* over My people Israel. And I will subdue all your enemies. Moreover, I tell you that the Lord will build a house for you. ¹¹ "When your days are fulfilled that you must go *to be* with your fathers, that I will set up *one of* your descendants after you, who will be of your sons; and I will establish his kingdom. ¹² "He shall build

for Me a house, and I will establish his throne forever. ¹³ "I will be his father and he shall be My son; and I will not take My lovingkindness away from him, as I took it from him who was before you. ¹⁴ "But I will settle him in My house and in My kingdom forever, and his throne shall be established forever." ' " ¹⁵ According to all these words and according to all this vision, so Nathan spoke to David.

1 CHRONICLES 17:16–27

¹⁶ Then David the king went in and sat before the Lord and said, "Who am I, O Lord God, and what is my house that You have brought me this far? ¹⁷ "This was a small thing in Your eyes, O God; but You have spoken of Your servant's house for a great while to come, and have regarded me according to the standard of a man of high degree, O Lord God. ¹⁸ "What more can David still *say* to You concerning the honor *bestowed* on Your servant? For You know Your servant. ¹⁹ "O Lord, for Your servant's sake, and according to Your own heart, You have wrought all this greatness, to make known all these great things. ²⁰ "O Lord, there is none like You, nor is there any God besides You, according to all that we have heard with our ears. ²¹ "And what one nation in the earth is like Your people Israel, whom God went to redeem for Himself *as* a people, to make You a name by great and terrible things, in driving out nations from before Your people, whom You redeemed out of Egypt? ²² "For Your people Israel You made Your own people forever, and You, O Lord, became their God. ²³ "Now, O Lord, let the word that You have spoken concerning Your servant and concerning his house be established forever, and do as You have spoken. ²⁴

"Let Your name be established and magnified forever, saying, 'The Lord of hosts is the God of Israel, *even* a God to Israel; and the house of David Your servant is established before You.' ²⁵ "For You, O my God, have revealed to Your servant that You will build for him a house; therefore Your servant has found *courage* to pray before You. ²⁶ "Now, O Lord, You are God, and have promised this good thing to Your servant. ²⁷ "And now it has pleased You to bless the house of Your servant, that it may continue forever before You; for You, O Lord, have blessed, and it is blessed forever."

1 CHRONICLES 22

¹ Then David said, "This is the house of the Lord God, and this is the altar of burnt offering for Israel." ² So David gave orders to gather the foreigners who were in the land of Israel, and he set stonecutters to hew out stones to build the house of God. ³ David prepared large quantities of iron to make the nails for the doors of the gates and for the clamps, and more bronze than could be weighed; ⁴ and timbers of cedar logs beyond number, for the Sidonians and Tyrians brought large quantities of cedar timber to David. ⁵ David said, "My son Solomon is young and inexperienced, and the house that is to be built for the Lord shall be exceedingly magnificent, famous and glorious throughout all lands. *Therefore* now I will make preparation for it." So David made ample preparations before his death. ⁶ Then he called for his son Solomon, and charged him to build a house for the Lord God of Israel. ⁷ David said to Solomon, "My son, I had intended to build a house to the name of the Lord my God. ⁸ "But the word of the Lord came to me, saying, 'You have shed much blood

and have waged great wars; you shall not build a house to My name, because you have shed *so* much blood on the earth before Me. ⁹'Behold, a son will be born to you, who shall be a man of rest; and I will give him rest from all his enemies on every side; for his name shall be Solomon, and I will give peace and quiet to Israel in his days. ¹⁰'He shall build a house for My name, and he shall be My son and I will be his father; and I will establish the throne of his kingdom over Israel forever.' ¹¹"Now, my son, the Lord be with you that you may be successful, and build the house of the Lord your God just as He has spoken concerning you. ¹²"Only the Lord give you discretion and understanding, and give you charge over Israel, so that you may keep the law of the Lord your God. ¹³"Then you will prosper, if you are careful to observe the statutes and the ordinances which the Lord commanded Moses concerning Israel. Be strong and courageous, do not fear nor be dismayed. ¹⁴"Now behold, with great pains I have prepared for the house of the Lord 100,000 talents of gold and 1,000,000 talents of silver, and bronze and iron beyond weight, for they are in great quantity; also timber and stone I have prepared, and you may add to them. ¹⁵"Moreover, there are many workmen with you, stonecutters and masons of stone and carpenters, and all men who are skillful in every kind of work. ¹⁶"Of the gold, the silver and the bronze and the iron there is no limit. Arise and work, and may the Lord be with you." ¹⁷David also commanded all the leaders of Israel to help his son Solomon, *saying,* ¹⁸"Is not the Lord your God with you? And has He not given you rest on every side? For He has given the inhabitants of the land into my hand, and the land is subdued before the Lord and before

His people. [19] "Now set your heart and your soul to seek the Lord your God; arise, therefore, and build the sanctuary of the Lord God, so that you may bring the ark of the covenant of the Lord and the holy vessels of God into the house that is to be built for the name of the Lord."

PSALM 40:1–3
[1] For the choir director. A Psalm of David. I waited patiently for the Lord; And He inclined to me and heard my cry. [2] He brought me up out of the pit of destruction, out of the miry clay, And He set my feet upon a rock making my footsteps firm. [3] He put a new song in my mouth, a song of praise to our God; Many will see and fear And will trust in the Lord.

ISAIAH 30:18
[18] Therefore the Lord longs to be gracious to you, And therefore He waits on high to have compassion on you. For the Lord is a God of justice; How blessed are all those who long for Him.

DANIEL 12:12
[12] "How blessed is he who keeps waiting and attains to the 1,335 days!

LAMENTATIONS 3:25
[25] The Lord is good to those who wait for Him, To the person who seeks Him.

PSALM 25:1–3
[1] *A Psalm* of David. To You, O Lord, I lift up my soul. [2] O my God, in You I trust, Do not let me be ashamed; Do not let my enemies exult over me. [3] Indeed, none of those who

wait for You will be ashamed; Those who deal treacherously without cause will be ashamed.

ISAIAH 49:23

[23] "Kings will be your guardians, And their princesses your nurses. They will bow down to you with their faces to the earth And lick the dust of your feet; And *you* will know that I am the Lord; Those who hopefully wait for Me will not be put to shame.

ISAIAH 40:31

[31] Yet those who wait for the Lord Will gain new strength; They will mount up *with* wings like eagles, They will run and not get tired, They will walk and not become weary.

PSALM 37:9

[9] For evildoers will be cut off, But those who wait for the Lord, they will inherit the land.

PROVERBS 20:22

[22] Do not say, "I will repay evil"; Wait for the Lord, and He will save you.

☸ CHAPTER 9

DEUTERONOMY 28

[1] "Now it shall be, if you diligently obey the Lord your God, being careful to do all His commandments which I command you today, the Lord your God will set you high above all the nations of the earth. [2] "All these blessings will come upon you and overtake you if you obey the Lord your God: [3] "Blessed *shall* you *be* in the city, and blessed *shall* you *be* in the

country. [4] "Blessed *shall be* the offspring of your body and the produce of your ground and the offspring of your beasts, the increase of your herd and the young of your flock. [5] "Blessed *shall be* your basket and your kneading bowl. [6] "Blessed *shall* you *be* when you come in, and blessed *shall* you *be* when you go out. [7] "The Lord shall cause your enemies who rise up against you to be defeated before you; they will come out against you one way and will flee before you seven ways. [8] "The Lord will command the blessing upon you in your barns and in all that you put your hand to, and He will bless you in the land which the Lord your God gives you. [9] "The Lord will establish you as a holy people to Himself, as He swore to you, if you keep the commandments of the Lord your God and walk in His ways. [10] "So all the peoples of the earth will see that you are called by the name of the Lord, and they will be afraid of you. [11] "The Lord will make you abound in prosperity, in the offspring of your body and in the offspring of your beast and in the produce of your ground, in the land which the Lord swore to your fathers to give you. [12] "The Lord will open for you His good storehouse, the heavens, to give rain to your land in its season and to bless all the work of your hand; and you shall lend to many nations, but you shall not borrow. [13] "The Lord will make you the head and not the tail, and you only will be above, and you will not be underneath, if you listen to the commandments of the Lord your God, which I charge you today, to observe *them* carefully, [14] and do not turn aside from any of the words which I command you today, to the right or to the left, to go after other gods to serve them. [15] "But it shall come about, if you do not obey the Lord your God, to observe to do all His commandments and His statutes with which I charge you today, that all these curses will come upon you and overtake you: ¹⁶ "Cursed *shall* you *be* in the city, and cursed *shall* you *be* in the country. ¹⁷ "Cursed *shall be* your basket and your kneading bowl. ¹⁸ "Cursed *shall be* the offspring of your body and the produce of your ground, the increase of your herd and the young of your flock. ¹⁹ "Cursed *shall* you *be* when you come in, and cursed *shall* you *be* when you go out. ²⁰ "The Lord will send upon you curses, confusion, and rebuke, in all you undertake to do, until you are destroyed and until you perish quickly, on account of the evil of your deeds, because you have forsaken Me. ²¹ "The Lord will make the pestilence cling to you until He has consumed you from the land where you are entering to possess it. ²² "The Lord will smite you with consumption and with fever and with inflammation and with fiery heat and with the sword and with blight and with mildew, and they will pursue you until you perish. ²³ "The heaven which is over your head shall be bronze, and the earth which is under you, iron. ²⁴ "The Lord will make the rain of your land powder and dust; from heaven it shall come down on you until you are destroyed. ²⁵ "The Lord shall cause you to be defeated before your enemies; you will go out one way against them, but you will flee seven ways before them, and you will be *an example of* terror to all the kingdoms of the earth. ²⁶ "Your carcasses will be food to all birds of the sky and to the beasts of the earth, and there will be no one to frighten *them* away. ²⁷ "The Lord will smite you with the boils of Egypt and with tumors and with the scab and with the itch, from which you cannot be healed. ²⁸ "The Lord will smite you with madness and with blindness and with bewilderment of heart; ²⁹ and you will grope at noon, as the blind man gropes in darkness, and you will not prosper in your ways; but you shall only be oppressed and robbed continually, with none to save you. ³⁰ "You shall betroth a wife, but another man will violate her; you shall build a house, but you will not live in it; you shall plant a vineyard, but you will not use its fruit. ³¹ "Your ox shall be slaughtered before your eyes, but you will not eat of it; your donkey shall be torn away from you, and will not be restored to you; your sheep shall be given to your enemies, and you will have none to save you. ³² "Your sons and your daughters shall be given to another people, while your eyes look on and yearn for them continually; but there will be nothing you can do. ³³ "A people whom you do not know shall eat up the produce of your ground and all your labors, and you will never be anything but oppressed and crushed continually. ³⁴ "You shall be driven mad by the sight of what you see. ³⁵ "The Lord will strike you on the knees and legs with sore boils, from which you cannot be healed, from the sole of your foot to the crown of your head. ³⁶ "The Lord will bring you and your king, whom you set over you, to a nation which neither you nor your fathers have known, and there you shall serve other gods, wood and stone. ³⁷ "You shall become a horror, a proverb, and a taunt among all the people where the Lord drives you. ³⁸ "You shall bring out much seed to the field but you will gather in little, for the locust will consume it. ³⁹ "You shall plant and cultivate vineyards, but you will neither drink of the wine nor gather *the grapes*, for the worm will devour them. ⁴⁰ "You shall have olive trees throughout your territory but you will not anoint yourself with the oil, for your olives will drop off. ⁴¹ "You shall have sons and daughters but they will not be yours, for they will go into captivity. ⁴² "The cricket shall possess all your trees and the produce of your ground. ⁴³ "The alien who is among you shall rise above you higher and higher, but you will go down lower and lower. ⁴⁴ "He shall lend to you, but you will not lend to him; he shall be the head, and you will be the tail. ⁴⁵ "So all these curses shall come on you and pursue you and overtake you until you are destroyed, because you would not obey the Lord your God by keeping His commandments and His statutes which He commanded you. ⁴⁶ "They shall become a sign and a wonder on you and your descendants forever. ⁴⁷ "Because you did not serve the Lord your God with joy and a glad heart, for the abundance of all things; ⁴⁸ therefore you shall serve your enemies whom the Lord will send against you, in hunger, in thirst, in nakedness, and in the lack of all things; and He will put an iron yoke on your neck until He has destroyed you. ⁴⁹ "The Lord will bring a nation against you from afar, from the end of the earth, as the eagle swoops down, a nation whose language you shall not understand, ⁵⁰ a nation of fierce countenance who will have no respect for the old, nor show favor to the young. ⁵¹ "Moreover, it shall eat the offspring of your herd and the produce of your ground until you are destroyed, who also leaves you no grain, new wine, or oil, nor the increase of your herd or the young of your flock until they have caused you to perish. ⁵² "It shall besiege you in all your towns until your high and fortified walls in which you trusted come down throughout your land, and it shall besiege you in all your towns throughout your land which the Lord your God has given you. ⁵³ "Then you shall eat the offspring of your own body, the flesh of your sons and of your daughters whom the Lord your God has given you, during the siege and the distress by which your enemy will oppress you. 54 "The man who is refined and very delicate among you shall be hostile toward his brother and toward the wife he cherishes and toward the rest of his children who remain, 55 so that he will not give *even* one of them any of the flesh of his children which he will eat, since he has nothing *else* left, during the siege and the distress by which your enemy will oppress you in all your towns. 56 "The refined and delicate woman among you, who would not venture to set the sole of her foot on the ground for delicateness and refinement, shall be hostile toward the husband she cherishes and toward her son and daughter, 57 and toward her afterbirth which issues from between her legs and toward her children whom she bears; for she will eat them secretly for lack of anything *else,* during the siege and the distress by which your enemy will oppress you in your towns. 58 "If you are not careful to observe all the words of this law which are written in this book, to fear this honored and awesome name, the Lord your God, 59 then the Lord will bring extraordinary plagues on you and your descendants, even severe and lasting plagues, and miserable and chronic sicknesses. 60 "He will bring back on you all the diseases of Egypt of which you were afraid, and they will cling to you. 61 "Also every sickness and every plague which, not written in the book of this law, the Lord will bring on you until you are destroyed. 62 "Then you shall be left few in number, whereas you were as numerous as the stars of heaven, because you did not obey the Lord your God. 63 "It shall come about that as the Lord delighted over you to prosper you, and multiply you, so the Lord will delight over you to make you perish and destroy you; and you will be torn from the land where you are entering to possess it. ⁶⁴ "Moreover, the Lord will scatter you among all peoples, from one end of the earth to the other end of the earth; and there you shall serve other gods, wood and stone, which you or your fathers have not known. ⁶⁵ "Among those nations you shall find no rest, and there will be no resting place for the sole of your foot; but there the Lord will give you a trembling heart, failing of eyes, and despair of soul. ⁶⁶ "So your life shall hang in doubt before you; and you will be in dread night and day, and shall have no assurance of your life. ⁶⁷ "In the morning you shall say, 'Would that it were evening!' And at evening you shall say, 'Would that it were morning!' because of the dread of your heart which you dread, and for the sight of your eyes which you will see. ⁶⁸ "The Lord will bring you back to Egypt in ships, by the way about which I spoke to you, 'You will never see it again!' And there you will offer yourselves for sale to your enemies as male and female slaves, but there will be no buyer."

2 SAMUEL 11

¹ Then it happened in the spring, at the time when kings go out *to battle,* that David sent Joab and his servants with him and all Israel, and they destroyed the sons of Ammon and besieged Rabbah. But David stayed at Jerusalem. ² Now when evening came David arose from his bed and walked around on the roof of the king's house, and from the roof he saw a woman bathing; and the woman was very beautiful in appearance. ³ So David sent and inquired about the woman. And one said, "Is this not Bathsheba, the daughter

of Eliam, the wife of Uriah the Hittite?" ⁴ David sent messengers and took her, and when she came to him, he lay with her; and when she had purified herself from her uncleanness, she returned to her house. ⁵ The woman conceived; and she sent and told David, and said, "I am pregnant." ⁶ Then David sent to Joab, *saying,* "Send me Uriah the Hittite." So Joab sent Uriah to David. ⁷ When Uriah came to him, David asked concerning the welfare of Joab and the people and the state of the war. ⁸ Then David said to Uriah, "Go down to your house, and wash your feet." And Uriah went out of the king's house, and a present from the king was sent out after him. ⁹ But Uriah slept at the door of the king's house with all the servants of his lord, and did not go down to his house. ¹⁰ Now when they told David, saying, "Uriah did not go down to his house," David said to Uriah, "Have you not come from a journey? Why did you not go down to your house?" ¹¹ Uriah said to David, "The ark and Israel and Judah are staying in temporary shelters, and my lord Joab and the servants of my lord are camping in the open field. Shall I then go to my house to eat and to drink and to lie with my wife? By your life and the life of your soul, I will not do this thing." ¹² Then David said to Uriah, "Stay here today also, and tomorrow I will let you go." So Uriah remained in Jerusalem that day and the next. ¹³ Now David called him, and he ate and drank before him, and he made him drunk; and in the evening he went out to lie on his bed with his lord's servants, but he did not go down to his house. ¹⁴ Now in the morning David wrote a letter to Joab and sent *it* by the hand of Uriah. ¹⁵ He had written in the letter, saying, "Place Uriah in the front line of the fiercest battle and withdraw from him, so that he may be struck down and die." ¹⁶ So it was as Joab kept watch on the city, that he put Uriah at the place where he knew there *were* valiant men. ¹⁷ The men of the city went out and fought against Joab, and some of the people among David's servants fell; and Uriah the Hittite also died. ¹⁸ Then Joab sent and reported to David all the events of the war. ¹⁹ He charged the messenger, saying, "When you have finished telling all the events of the war to the king, ²⁰ and if it happens that the king's wrath rises and he says to you, 'Why did you go so near to the city to fight? Did you not know that they would shoot from the wall? ²¹ 'Who struck down Abimelech the son of Jerubbesheth? Did not a woman throw an upper millstone on him from the wall so that he died at Thebez? Why did you go so near the wall?'—then you shall say, 'Your servant Uriah the Hittite is dead also.' " ²² So the messenger departed and came and reported to David all that Joab had sent him *to tell*. ²³ The messenger said to David, "The men prevailed against us and came out against us in the field, but we pressed them as far as the entrance of the gate. ²⁴ "Moreover, the archers shot at your servants from the wall; so some of the king's servants are dead, and your servant Uriah the Hittite is also dead." ²⁵ Then David said to the messenger, "Thus you shall say to Joab, 'Do not let this thing displease you, for the sword devours one as well as another; make your battle against the city stronger and overthrow it'; and *so* encourage him." ²⁶ Now when the wife of Uriah heard that Uriah her husband was dead, she mourned for her husband. ²⁷ When the *time of* mourning was over, David sent and brought her to his house and she became his wife; then she bore him a son. But the thing that David had done was evil in the sight of the Lord.

[1]Then the Lord sent Nathan to David. And he came to him and said, "There were two men in one city, the one rich and the other poor. [2]"The rich man had a great many flocks and herds. [3]"But the poor man had nothing except one little ewe lamb Which he bought and nourished; And it grew up together with him and his children. It would eat of his bread and drink of his cup and lie in his bosom, And was like a daughter to him. [4]"Now a traveler came to the rich man, And he was unwilling to take from his own flock or his own herd, To prepare for the wayfarer who had come to him; Rather he took the poor man's ewe lamb and prepared it for the man who had come to him." [5]Then David's anger burned greatly against the man, and he said to Nathan, "As the Lord lives, surely the man who has done this deserves to die. [6]"He must make restitution for the lamb fourfold, because he did this thing and had no compassion." [7]Nathan then said to David, "You are the man! Thus says the Lord God of Israel, 'It is I who anointed you king over Israel and it is I who delivered you from the hand of Saul. [8]'I also gave you your master's house and your master's wives into your care, and I gave you the house of Israel and Judah; and if *that had been* too little, I would have added to you many more things like these! [9]'Why have you despised the word of the Lord by doing evil in His sight? You have struck down Uriah the Hittite with the sword, have taken his wife to be your wife, and have killed him with the sword of the sons of Ammon. [10]'Now there-

174 | *Debbie Blough*

fore, the sword shall never depart from your house, because you have despised Me and have taken the wife of Uriah the Hittite to be your wife.' " "Thus says the Lord, 'Behold, I will raise up evil against you from your own household; I will even take your wives before your eyes and give *them* to your companion, and he will lie with your wives in broad daylight. ¹² 'Indeed you did it secretly, but I will do this thing before all Israel, and under the sun.' " ¹³ Then David said to Nathan, "I have sinned against the Lord." And Nathan said to David, "The Lord also has taken away your sin; you shall not die. ¹⁴ "However, because by this deed you have given occasion to the enemies of the Lord to blaspheme, the child also that is born to you shall surely die."

2 SAMUEL 12:15–23

¹⁵ So Nathan went to his house. Then the Lord struck the child that Uriah's widow bore to David, so that he was *very* sick. ¹⁶ David therefore inquired of God for the child; and David fasted and went and lay all night on the ground. ¹⁷ The elders of his household stood beside him in order to raise him up from the ground, but he was unwilling and would not eat food with them. ¹⁸ Then it happened on the seventh day that the child died. And the servants of David were afraid to tell him that the child was dead, for they said, "Behold, while the child was *still* alive, we spoke to him and he did not listen to our voice. How then can we tell him that the child is dead, since he might do *himself* harm!" ¹⁹ But when David saw that his servants were whispering together, David perceived that the child was dead; so David said to his servants, "Is the child dead?" And they said, "He is dead." ²⁰ So David arose from

the ground, washed, anointed *himself*, and changed his clothes; and he came into the house of the Lord and worshiped. Then he came to his own house, and when he requested, they set food before him and he ate. ²¹ Then his servants said to him, "What is this thing that you have done? While the child was alive, you fasted and wept; but when the child died, you arose and ate food." ²² He said, "While the child was *still* alive, I fasted and wept; for I said, 'Who knows, the Lord may be gracious to me, that the child may live.' ²³ "But now he has died; why should I fast? Can I bring him back again? I will go to him, but he will not return to me."

⚜ CHAPTER 10

JOB 1:20–22

²⁰ Then Job arose and tore his robe and shaved his head, and he fell to the ground and worshiped. ²¹ He said, "Naked I came from my mother's womb, And naked I shall return there. The Lord gave and the Lord has taken away. Blessed be the name of the Lord." ²² Through all this Job did not sin nor did he blame God.

DANIEL 4:9–27

⁹ 'O Belteshazzar, chief of the magicians, since I know that a spirit of the holy gods is in you and no mystery baffles you, tell *me* the visions of my dream which I have seen, along with its interpretation. ¹⁰ 'Now *these were* the visions in my mind *as I lay* on my bed: I was looking, and behold, *there was* a tree in the midst of the earth and its height *was* great. ¹¹ 'The tree grew large and became strong And its height reached to the sky, And it *was* visible to the end of the whole earth.

¹² 'Its foliage *was* beautiful and its fruit abundant, And in it *was* food for all. The beasts of the field found shade under it, And the birds of the sky dwelt in its branches, And all living creatures fed themselves from it. ¹³ 'I was looking in the visions in my mind *as I lay* on my bed, and behold, an *angelic* watcher, a holy one, descended from heaven. ¹⁴ 'He shouted out and spoke as follows: "Chop down the tree and cut off its branches, Strip off its foliage and scatter its fruit; Let the beasts flee from under it And the birds from its branches. ¹⁵ "Yet leave the stump with its roots in the ground, But with a band of iron and bronze *around it* In the new grass of the field; And let him be drenched with the dew of heaven, And let him share with the beasts in the grass of the earth. ¹⁶ "Let his mind be changed from *that of* a man And let a beast's mind be given to him, And let seven periods of time pass over him. ¹⁷ "This sentence is by the decree of the *angelic* watchers And the decision is a command of the holy ones, In order that the living may know That the Most High is ruler over the realm of mankind, And bestows it on whom He wishes And sets over it the lowliest of men." ¹⁸ 'This is the dream *which* I, King Nebuchadnezzar, have seen. Now you, Belteshazzar, tell *me* its interpretation, inasmuch as none of the wise men of my kingdom is able to make known to me the interpretation; but you are able, for a spirit of the holy gods is in you.' ¹⁹ "Then Daniel, whose name is Belteshazzar, was appalled for a while as his thoughts alarmed him. The king responded and said, 'Belteshazzar, do not let the dream or its interpretation alarm you.' Belteshazzar replied, 'My lord, *if only* the dream applied to those who hate you and its interpretation to your adversaries! ²⁰ 'The tree that you saw,

which became large and grew strong, whose height reached to the sky and was visible to all the earth ²¹ and whose foliage *was* beautiful and its fruit abundant, and in which *was* food for all, under which the beasts of the field dwelt and in whose branches the birds of the sky lodged—²² it is you, O king; for you have become great and grown strong, and your majesty has become great and reached to the sky and your dominion to the end of the earth. ²³ 'In that the king saw an *angelic* watcher, a holy one, descending from heaven and saying, "Chop down the tree and destroy it; yet leave the stump with its roots in the ground, but with a band of iron and bronze *around it* in the new grass of the field, and let him be drenched with the dew of heaven, and let him share with the beasts of the field until seven periods of time pass over him," ²⁴ this is the interpretation, O king, and this is the decree of the Most High, which has come upon my lord the king: ²⁵ that you be driven away from mankind and your dwelling place be with the beasts of the field, and you be given grass to eat like cattle and be drenched with the dew of heaven; and seven periods of time will pass over you, until you recognize that the Most High is ruler over the realm of mankind and bestows it on whomever He wishes. ²⁶ 'And in that it was commanded to leave the stump with the roots of the tree, your kingdom will be assured to you after you recognize that *it is* Heaven *that* rules. ²⁷ 'Therefore, O king, may my advice be pleasing to you: break away now from your sins by *doing* righteousness and from your iniquities by showing mercy to *the* poor, in case there may be a prolonging of your prosperity.'

²⁹ "Twelve months later he was walking on the *roof of* the royal palace of Babylon. ³⁰ "The king reflected and said, 'Is this not Babylon the great, which I myself have built as a royal residence by the might of my power and for the glory of my majesty?'

³¹ "While the word *was* in the king's mouth, a voice came from heaven, *saying*, 'King Nebuchadnezzar, to you it is declared: sovereignty has been removed from you, ³² and you will be driven away from mankind, and your dwelling place *will be* with the beasts of the field. You will be given grass to eat like cattle, and seven periods of time will pass over you until you recognize that the Most High is ruler over the realm of mankind and bestows it on whomever He wishes.' ³³ "Immediately the word concerning Nebuchadnezzar was fulfilled; and he was driven away from mankind and began eating grass like cattle, and his body was drenched with the dew of heaven until his hair had grown like eagles' *feathers* and his nails like birds' *claws.* ³⁴ "But at the end of that period, I, Nebuchadnezzar, raised my eyes toward heaven and my reason returned to me, and I blessed the Most High and praised and honored Him who lives forever; For His dominion is an everlasting dominion, And His kingdom *endures* from generation to generation. ³⁵ "All the inhabitants of the earth are accounted as nothing, But He does according to His will in the host of heaven And *among* the inhabitants of earth; And no one can ward off His hand Or say to Him, 'What have You done?' ³⁶ "At that time my reason returned

to me. And my majesty and splendor were restored to me for the glory of my kingdom, and my counselors and my nobles began seeking me out; so I was reestablished in my sovereignty, and surpassing greatness was added to me. [37] "Now I, Nebuchadnezzar, praise, exalt and honor the King of heaven, for all His works are true and His ways just, and He is able to humble those who walk in pride."

JAMES 1:16–17

[16] Do not be deceived, my beloved brethren. [17] Every good thing given and every perfect gift is from above, coming down from the Father of lights, with whom there is no variation or shifting shadow.

MATTHEW 5:45

[45] so that you may be sons of your Father who is in heaven; for He causes His sun to rise on *the* evil and *the* good, and sends rain on *the* righteous and *the* unrighteous.

MATTHEW 7:13–14

[13] "Enter through the narrow gate; for the gate is wide and the way is broad that leads to destruction, and there are many who enter through it. [14] "For the gate is small and the way is narrow that leads to life, and there are few who find it.

ROMANS 3:10–12

[10] as it is written, "There is none righteous, not even one; [11] There is none who understands, There is none who seeks for God; [12] All have turned aside, together they have become useless; There is none who does good, There is not even one."

ROMANS 3:23

²³ for all have sinned and fall short of the glory of God,

NUMBERS 21:4–9

⁴ Then they set out from Mount Hor by the way of the Red Sea, to go around the land of Edom; and the people became impatient because of the journey. ⁵ The people spoke against God and Moses, "Why have you brought us up out of Egypt to die in the wilderness? For there is no food and no water, and we loathe this miserable food." ⁶ The Lord sent fiery serpents among the people and they bit the people, so that many people of Israel died. ⁷ So the people came to Moses and said, "We have sinned, because we have spoken against the Lord and you; intercede with the Lord, that He may remove the serpents from us." And Moses interceded for the people. ⁸ Then the Lord said to Moses, "Make a fiery *serpent,* and set it on a standard; and it shall come about, that everyone who is bitten, when he looks at it, he will live." ⁹ And Moses made a bronze serpent and set it on the standard; and it came about, that if a serpent bit any man, when he looked to the bronze serpent, he lived.

JOHN 3:14–15

¹⁴ "As Moses lifted up the serpent in the wilderness, even so must the Son of Man be lifted up; ¹⁵ so that whoever believes will in Him have eternal life.

2 CORINTHIANS 5:21

²¹ He made Him who knew no sin *to be* sin on our behalf, so that we might become the righteousness of God in Him

LUKE 17:11–19

¹¹ While He was on the way to Jerusalem, He was passing between Samaria and Galilee. ¹² As He entered a village, ten leprous men who stood at a distance met Him; ¹³ and they raised their voices, saying, "Jesus, Master, have mercy on us!" ¹⁴ When He saw them, He said to them, "Go and show yourselves to the priests." And as they were going, they were cleansed. ¹⁵ Now one of them, when he saw that he had been healed, turned back, glorifying God with a loud voice, ¹⁶ and he fell on his face at His feet, giving thanks to Him. And he was a Samaritan. ¹⁷ Then Jesus answered and said, "Were there not ten cleansed? But the nine—where are they? ¹⁸ "Was no one found who returned to give glory to God, except this foreigner?" ¹⁹ And He said to him, "Stand up and go; your faith has made you well."

Melissa S.

Sovereign

to you?